All You Need to Know About...

Raising Girls

Melissa Trevathan
Sissy Goff

ZONDERVAN®

ZONDERVAN

Raising Girls

Requests for information should be addressed to:

Zondervan, *Grand Rapids, Michigan 49530*

Library of Congress Cataloging-in-Publication Data

Trevathan, Melissa, 1950-
Raising girls / Melissa Trevathan and Sissy Goff.
p. cm.
Includes bibliographical references and index.
ISBN 978-0-310-27289-2
1. Parenting—Religious aspects—Christianity. 2. Child rearing—Religious aspects—Christianity. 3. Girls. 4. Teenage girls. I. Goff, Sissy, 1970- II. Title.
BV4529.T745 2007
248.8'45—dc22 2006039536

Published in association with the literary agency of Alive Communications, Inc., 7680 Goddard Street, Suite 200, Colorado Springs, CO 80920. www.alivecommunications.com.

Interior design by Beth Shagene

Printed in the United States of America

Contents

For the girls who have helped raise us:
Kathleen, Mady, Libby, Olivia, Savannah,
Mary Dea, Mamie, Brittney, McClain,
Anne Mason, Ellie, Meredith Laine,
Anna Grace, Mary Holland, Noel, Molasses,
and all of the Daystar interns and girls
who are too many to mention but have offered
their laughter and hearts to inspire this book.

Foreword by Cindy Morgan

A couple of Wednesdays ago, my three-year-old daughter, Savannah, and I were making the most of an overcast day off by doing chores. We cleaned my car and Savannah, being a generous and sweet-spirited girl, had offered to help.

In a comfortable silence with only the sound of the wind, the birds, and an occasional passing car, we worked. I vacuumed happy meal crumbs and wiped off leftover ice cream from the seats while Savannah attempted, with a small washcloth, to clean the outside of our large gas-guzzling SUV. She was so enormously proud of her work that she would stop every few minutes to proclaim "Mommy, look! I'm the best cleaner in the whole world!"

As any mother would, I heartily agreed, taking a moment each time to carefully examine her work before giving the well-deserved praise she was waiting for.

I watched her face as she cleaned, her golden brown hair a mess, wearing a well-worn princess gown. With tears welling up in my eyes, I said, "I love you, Savannah"

To my surprise, she said, "Why do you always say that?"

"Well . . . ," I said, taking a moment to meet her question with a deserving answer, "I tell you because sometimes I feel so full of love that I have to let it out and let you know how I feel."

"You mean, you're afraid I'll forgot." (Yes, she said, "forgot.")

"That's right, babe, I want to make sure you know all the time."

"Okay," she said, " I know."

☆

When I met Sissy and Melissa about fifteen years ago, long before I was married, they were women who cared deeply for me, my life, my spirit, and my happiness. My first memory of Sissy was her watching my attempt to assemble my new TV stand and VCR. She barely knew me, but as I sat there, overwhelmed in a pile of nuts and bolts, trying to make sense of the directions, Sissy said with that beautiful smile she has, "Let me help." And she did.

I met Melissa one summer not long after that, when we all decided to watch a TV miniseries called *Matthew*. Some of us girls would meet at Melissa's cozy cottage in Greenhills and talk about life, boys, and other mysteries of the world and eat as much ice cream as possible. To be with Melissa was, in some ways, like being with one of the great women in the Bible. She has a calming, wise presence, communicating that everything is gonna be okay because God's in control.

Melissa would ask me to tell stories about my childhood in east Tennessee, which would usually lead to stories about my own tumultuous relationship with my mother.

Savannah and I are still at that wonderful time in life where she wants to know what I think. She wants me to read her stories and spend as much time as possible bundled in my arms playing I-spy. I know that will change soon as it already has with my six-year-old, Olivia.

Olivia is our drama queen, our diva/tomgirl. We wouldn't change her for anything, but at times I'm pushed beyond the limits of my parenting skills. In a way, she and I are much like my mother and I were. Gratefully, through much help and encouragement, my mom and I have been able to wade through a lot of our issues.

There have been many times over the years that I've called Melissa and Sissy to ask their thoughts on my relationship with my mother and my girls. Long before they began writing this book, they were living out its pages, being there in hard times with tears and late night calls. They were always there to shed light on the questions that seem so hard and mysterious. They bring the love of God, combined with a tremendous amount of dedication, experience, and a divine purpose to not only offer answers for raising our kids but to shed light on the child inside us who wants the answers that never came as a child.

My mother, my girls, even I, need to be reminded that we are strong. That we are smart. That we are loved. Like Savannah more often that not, I think we "forgot."

My husband and I asked Sissy to be Olivia's godmother and Melissa to be Savannah's (or "fairy godmothers," as my girls call them). On holidays, special occasions, or sometimes no occasion at all, they will come to our house with thoughtful gifts and spend time with our girls, carving pumpkins, coloring pages, or assembling life-size dollhouses. I'm not sure what my life would be like without them.

I've often heard it said how strange it is that you need training to drive a car you but no training is required to be a parent. Sadly, many of our children take the fall for that.

I'm so grateful for this book—for the hours, months, weeks, and years and years of conversations with girls that have helped Sissy and Melissa understand, so deeply and completely, what it feels like to be a girl and what tools their parents need to help girls grow into the beautiful, splendid creatures God intended them to be.

CINDY MORGAN
May 1, 2007

Raising Girls: An Introduction

That's what a girl is: potential. She knows few limits. A girl is strong. She knows little of fatigue, only her own boundless energy. A girl is a comrade of other girls, all hard at the business of becoming.

BARBARA CAWTHORNE CRAFTON, *THE SEWING ROOM*

"You're not as pretty as your sister, so you're going to have to learn to make something of yourself."

The eight-year-old girl who was told this is now eighty, and she has never forgotten it. She has spent the last seventy-two years trying to accomplish something that she—and ultimately her father—would be proud of.

Her father was unaware of his daughter's potential. Rather than calling out all of the good God had placed inside of her, he unwittingly used his greatest source of influence—his relationship with her—for harm.

Such unawareness is one reason we are writing this book. As countless parents have said to us, a girl doesn't come with an instruction manual, and raising the girl you love will be, by far, one of the most complicated jobs you will ever hold.

The purpose of this book, therefore, is to enlighten you, whether you're a parent, a grandparent, or some other adult in the life of a girl. We hope to offer insight as to why your daughter, who is six, says that she hates herself when she can't fix her hair just right. We want to help you know how to respond when your granddaughter comes home from school several days in a row in tears because she has been left out of her triangle of "friends." And we want to help you understand your niece, who the rest of the world thinks is delightful, when all you see is her rage and indifference.

Raising girls can be a daunting task, and in today's world it is daunting in different ways than ever before. For countless generations, girls have worried about who to sit with at lunch, what dress to wear to a dance, and what boy they are going to marry in twenty years. For many years they have also wrestled with such issues as depression, suicide, abuse, and eating disorders.

Today, however, things have taken a darker, more complex turn. Girls follow their friends to the bathroom to make sure they are not throwing up after lunch. Topics like *self-mutilation* and *Internet relationships* are a normal part of any parenting class for girls. The issues are much the same, but they are out in the open and seem to grow in intensity with each generation. Add to these the age-old issues of girls—the insecurities of adolescence, the meanness of middle school girls, and the dangers of high school boys—and you end up with more than a few concerned parents.

We see a lot of these parents in our offices. As counselors at a ministry for children and adolescents, we see children in grades two through twelve and their families. The children we see are dealing with a myriad of issues, most of which are prevalent in any school in any state in our country. They struggle with social issues such as being made fun of, family issues like divorce or loss of a family member, self-esteem issues, and issues involving self-destructive behaviors such as eating disorders and experimentation with alcohol, to name a few. Many families even come for preventive purposes. Whatever their reasons for coming to Daystar Counseling Ministries, these parents are probably much like you—concerned about the children they love and wanting our support in helping their children become who God has created them to be.

Raising Girls is divided into three parts based on the three main areas of concern we hear most often from parents:

Part One: What's Normal, What's Not?

We spend a great deal of time simply talking to parents about the developmental stages of girls, explaining what to expect as their daughters mature. Understanding the typical behaviors of any given stage of development can help you know that your daughter's behavior is not a sign of flawed character, but a normal part of her development.

Part Two: What's Going On with Her?

In this section, we take a deeper look at what is going on inside her heart and mind. We also look more closely at the culture around her and the pressures coming against her.

Part Three: How Can I Help?

Understanding what is going on in their lives helps us to better answer the final question—"How can I help?" This help comes in several forms. You help your daughter as you learn to believe in her, enjoy her, and see her clearly past the haze of your own fears. In this section, we hope to help you discover not only who God has created your daughter to be, but also how you can call out her unique identity—a process we refer to as "naming."

☆

Although these three parts are sequential, feel free to roam throughout the book. In Part One, we include information about your daughter's physical, spiritual, and emotional development at each of the four stages of development. The more preventive parent may read the entire book from cover to cover. Another parent may only read the chapters that pertain to his or her daughter. We would encourage you to do whatever feels most helpful to you.

Parts Two and Three, however, are helpful for any adult in the life of a girl. If your daughter is young, those sections will give you the foresight to know what to expect and the wisdom to handle it. If she's in middle or high school, you'll get a glimpse into all that she's *not* talking about: who she is, what she's thinking, and how you can help. We suggest reading these sections thoroughly.

You may be surprised to find not only your daughter but yourself in these pages. We hope you do. In counseling girls, we find the parents are just as much a part of the process as the girls themselves. *Raising Girls* explores the same principle. We want to provide practical and insightful tools as you raise your daughter, and we want to give you the encouragement and reassurance that helps you grow right alongside her.

We are blessed to be able to do this work year round. As counselors, we have a unique opportunity to have a voice in the lives of both the children and parents that walk through the doors of Daystar Counseling Ministries.

As children grow, the voices in their lives change in intensity. Usually the parental voices become quieter as other voices become louder. We say on a regular basis that, at Daystar, we are simply a new voice. We often tell children and adolescents the same things their parents have told them, but we are a different voice and are heard a little more loudly because of it.

We believe that parents need to hear other voices as well. Parenting is a challenging, delightful, heart-wrenching journey that can feel profoundly overwhelming and lonely at times. Parents need guides who understand the world of their children. These guides are much more effective when they have earned the trust of a child who will speak directly and honestly to them. We have the honor of being these guides within our community at Daystar.

Basically, we have a foot in the worlds of both parents and their children.

Melissa has been caring for children and adolescents since she was sixteen, when she first became a youth director. That makes almost forty years of loving, encouraging, and disrupting the lives of kids. Sissy has done the same, particularly with girls, for the past thirteen years. Combined, we see approximately fifty children and adolescents per week. Mathematically speaking, we have been able to have a voice in the lives of more than ten thousand children and adolescents—between the two of us.

This effectiveness would simply not be possible if we each had our own families. Because of our place in life, we are able to spend our summers with the children and adolescents that we counsel—and we are able to stand between the children and parents who come into our offices. Kids relate to us because we're not parents. Parents relate to us because we're adults and have spent years working with children and adolescents.

We believe our place in life works to our benefit. It gives our collective voice a definite credibility. We know what is going on in the lives of girls from having listened to the girls themselves—and a lot of them—and we know the struggles and joys of parenting because we sit with weary, concerned parents day in and day out.

You may be one of those weary and concerned parents. But we know without a doubt that God has specifically and purposefully chosen you to raise the girl you love. He has chosen you—precisely where you are and who you are—and not some perfected image of yourself. If you were a perfect parent, you would expect a perfect daughter—and that would cancel out any uniqueness contained within either one of you.

Therein lies the importance of this book. It is a journey into the hearts of girls, a journey that takes you through the world around her to the depths of what is happening inside her. It is designed to equip you with a voice to call out who God has uniquely created her to be.

It is our privilege to guide you in this process of raising girls. As you read, we hope you will ponder, wrestle, laugh, and discover the unique identity God has given your daughter ... and maybe even a little more of the identity he has given you.

PART ONE

What's Normal, What's Not

CHAPTER 1

What's Going On?

Aunt Em had just come out of the house to water the cabbages when she looked up and saw Dorothy running toward her.

"My darling child!" she cried, folding the little girl in her arms and covering her face with kisses. "Where in the world did you come from?"

"From the Land of Oz," said Dorothy gravely. "And here is Toto, too. And oh, Aunt Em! I'm so glad to be at home again!"

L. FRANK BAUM, *THE WIZARD OF OZ*

"I don't understand what's going on with my daughter. She used to want to talk to me when she came home from school. Now, I can't get her to come out of her room. I'm afraid she's depressed."

"All my daughter thinks about now is her friends. She won't go visit her grandparents. She doesn't practice piano anymore. She sits in front of her computer talking to six different kids at one time. She just seems so selfish."

"My daughter has developed an extremely frightening habit of lying. It can be about what she ate for lunch, a grade she got on a test, or how late she stayed out with her friends. It doesn't matter the seriousness of the situation – it's like she doesn't know a lie from the truth anymore."

These are just a few of the many worries we hear from parents every day. All these parents, at some level, look at their girls and say, "What's going on?" or, in the words of Aunt Em, "Where in the world did you come from?"

We talk with parents because they are concerned about their children. Sometimes something tragic has happened in the life of their child to make the parents believe they need to talk to someone. Sometimes parents just can't figure out what is going on in their child's life, but they know they need help. In the latter case, one word brings clarity to at least 60 percent of the situations: that word is *development.*

"Why does my daughter feel so bad about herself when nothing has happened?"

Development.

"Why is my toddler talking so much more than her brother did at the same age?"

Development.

"Why won't she let me help her with anything anymore?"

You guessed it—development.

We're not saying development is the culprit in every difficult situation in the life of a growing girl. But it sure makes a difference.

THE FOUR STAGES OF DEVELOPMENT

Development has been defined as "the bringing out of all that is potentially contained within." And whether your daughter is two, twelve, or twenty, what is contained within her ranges from wonderful to, at times, pretty nasty.

This is normal.

And it is completely normal to feel, at times, like someone has stolen the daughter you enjoyed five minutes ago and replaced her with a fire-breathing dragon with the same eyes.

In those moments you ask yourself, "What's going on?"

Part One answers that question. In this section, we look at the specifics of development. We examine what is going on in a girl's life physically, emotionally, and spiritually in each of four developmental stages. We also talk about what we, as adults, can offer her at every stage.

Stage 1: The Discovery Years—Birth to Five

In the Discovery Years, girls awaken to the world around them. They discover themselves as separate from their parents, and, in essence, they crawl, toddle, and walk away from you and toward their own identities.

Stage 2: The Adventurous Years—Six to Eleven

The Adventurous Years are filled with school, friends, and activities. Girls stretch their limits as they try new things and begin to learn what it means to succeed and to fail.

Stage 3: The Narcissistic Years—Twelve to Fifteen

These are the "me" years. The world of your daughter in her Narcissistic Years revolves around herself. Her thoughts are consumed by how she looks, what other people think about how she looks, and what other people think of her in general.

Stage 4: The Autonomous Years—Sixteen to Nineteen

In these years, girls take greater responsibility for and control of their lives. And they are able to find their own voices—what they are passionate about, who they choose to be in a relationship with, how they want to spend their time, and who God truly is creating them to be.

☆

For a parent, development is an emotional roller coaster. You have the joy of watching your thirteen-month-old daughter's first steps, but you also know that those steps make her more independent. You walk your six-year-old to the school bus for the first time, proud and tearful as she enters a world that doesn't involve you. Your heart drops as you come to the top of the stairs and watch your twelve-year-old jump up to shut her door, rather than to greet you. You swell with a mixture of fear, longing, and hope for your sixteen-year-old as she drives away by herself for the first time. Finally, your girl in her blue check dress comes running to you with her dog, Toto. You fold her in your arms and say, "My darling child, where in the world did you come from?" And she is simply glad to be home.

Development is a journey—a journey all girls will pass through in their birth-to-nineteen years (and on up, for most of us). At each stage, God is teaching girls something valuable about who they are, and he is allowing them to learn, by trial and error, characteristics that will help them navigate their adult years.

GETTING STUCK

If your daughter didn't move through each of these important stages of development, she would never learn to separate from you and become the unique woman God is calling her to be.

Girls can become stuck in their development. Often, trauma in the life of a maturing girl or boy can cause that child to stall—to never move beyond a particular developmental stage. This can be crippling in their later lives.

We have a friend who grew up in a small town in Eastern Europe. Her mother died during childbirth, and her father was in international business. She grew up speaking a different language and in a culture where clothes had nothing to do with status.

When our friend was in the sixth grade, her father met a woman on a business trip to the United States. He decided to marry this woman and raise his family in America. Our friend started seventh grade in Dallas, Texas. She had no social awareness. She had never heard the word *popular*, let alone worried about whether she was or not. As you can imagine, her world changed dramatically in a few days.

This friend continues to have difficulty in relationships. She is socially awkward and has a very immature sense of humor. If she gets close to someone, she sabotages the relationship. Believing that arguing is what makes friends close, she sets up arguments with her friends. Obviously, her friends tire of her quickly.

Relationally this young woman is still living in the seventh grade. She got stuck at that age and has yet to move beyond it. Any of us can become stuck at different places in our development—and we all probably have at some point or another.

As you read the chapters on development, you may read about milestones you never reached, or you may hear suggestions for parents that your parents never offered you.

There is hope. Even when our parents fail, even when you fail as a parent (which you will . . . often), we have a perfect parent. As our Father, God desires to use our development not only to help call out who we were created to be, but to draw us closer to him. He doesn't require our perfection or the perfection of our imperfect pasts to equip us to be parents.

As you read this section, think not only about your daughter's past but also about your own. Where do you see yourself in terms of your development in each particular chapter? Where could you have possibly gotten stuck? Can you see how this "stuck-ness" could affect your own parenting? Can you see how it affects your view of yourself or your close relationships?

In the last section of the book, we talk further about the importance of looking at your own life. We would like you to do this as you read the entire book:

- Read a little
- Put it down
- Talk to your spouse or a friend
- Pray about what God is teaching you about your daughter
- Pray about what he wants to say to you about your own life

☆

Neither your development nor your daughter's is fully over until you reach heaven. To help you understand more of what your girl is going through, remember your own development—the successes and failures, the stresses and strains, that defined those years.

Raising girls and helping call out who God is creating them to be is a difficult task. It is especially difficult in light of so much of what is brought out during their developing years. In reality, what we see in them is not so different than what our parents saw in us. To know that these things are normal—that they are a part of the development not just of your daughter, but of every girl—makes the process a little easier.

CHAPTER 2

The Discovery Years: Birth to Five

Just to watch a child at this work of exploring every detail of some perfectly ordinary physical object — this is an act of contemplation, which itself has a sanctifying effect upon the observer.... I need a child to teach me once more how magical the world is, how everything that exists is charged with an overpowering enchantment.

MIKE MASON, *THE MYSTERY OF CHILDREN*

I (Sissy) rarely lost my temper as a teenager. But one night, for some reason that was significant to me at fifteen and I haven't a clue about today, I did. I remember yelling at my parents, ranting and raving and throwing my hairbrush as hard as I could into my mirror. I went to bed in tears with the promise that I would never speak to either one of them again.

The next morning my dad told me I needed to come straight home from school so we could all talk. I came home that afternoon and was invited into the bedroom with my very serious-looking parents. Through the haze of words directed at me by my dad, I kept expecting to hear the words *disrespect* and *grounded*. Instead, I heard just one — *baby*. I had to ask them to repeat themselves several times. "Your mother is going to have a baby." My mom swears the next thing I said was, "I didn't think you all did that anymore."

Well, they did. On July 7 of the following year, I had a beautiful baby sister named Kathleen. My parents were delighted, and I was excited to have their attention focused on someone else during my first summer holding keys to a car.

I had never been around babies before. So, I parked my car every once in a while to play with Kathleen. Actually, I thought I would play with her, but she didn't play. From my sixteen-year-old perspective, she didn't do anything. Mom and Dad were as excited when she smiled or made a gurgly noise as they were when I brought home an A on my report card. I didn't really get it. I remember telling my mom often, "She's kind of boring. I'm ready for her to do something."

While I thought all Kathleen was doing was lying there with a cute smile, dirtying her diapers, her brain was forming lightning-fast connections. She was learning to differentiate sights and sounds, she was developing her own little personality, and she was beginning to conceptualize God in her own babylike way.

DISCOVERY IN ACTION

Children ages birth to five perform countless monumental tasks on a daily basis in this stage of their lives. Every day for a baby is a crash course in life as her brain forms new neural pathways. She sees and feels and hears and smells (and tastes, unfortunately) new objects with every passing hour. Babies and toddlers are learning about relationships, trust, hope, independence, attachment, and countless other concepts that we adults spend the rest of our lifetimes trying to understand. A girl in the birth-to-five-year-old stage is discovery in action. She is learning to crawl, to pull herself up, to walk, to speak.

It is exhausting even to think about all that goes on in the first five years of a girl's life, but it is tremendously helpful for them when we do. To help girls grow through those first five years, it is vitally important that we understand the development of their bodies, emotions and personalities, and spiritual lives.

PHYSICAL DEVELOPMENT

Our friend Mimi visited us while we were writing this chapter, to encourage us and spur us on. She brought us each a Starbucks and said, "Could you just finish it tonight? I'm tired of this chapter already."

"We're trying—we just got to the section on bodies," Melissa replied.

"What is there to say at this age?" asked Mimi. "They're just little and cute and squishy."

Mimi's right. They are little and very cute and very, very squishy. But as she knows, having raised three girls herself, they are a lot more too. It's hard for us to know what is happening to girls at this age because they can't verbalize all that is going on inside their brains. But a great deal is going on that is different from what is going on in the brains of boys. Girls' and boys' bodies may look similar, but what is happening inside their brains is entirely different. Because of the way God designed their brains to develop, girls and boys differ in four significant areas in the way they acquire skills during the Discovery Years.

Speech Development

Girls are more talkative than boys. This begins early and only slows down in adolescence—when it just seems as though girls are not as talkative because they're not talking to us. Once a girl starts to talk, the momentum builds rapidly. There is a very simple, biological reason for this—at least in our Discovery-age girls. All brains grow from the right hemisphere to the left. As the growth reaches the left hemisphere, girls and boys begin to speak. But since the left hemisphere of girls' brains develops earlier than boys', girls begin to speak earlier.

Impulse Control

In our group counseling sessions at Daystar, our colleagues David and Jeremy, who lead the boys' groups, often have to tell the boys to sit on their hands. These boys poke and jab each other as a natural way of relating to each other. They also have a great deal of difficulty controlling their impulses. In our girls' group counseling sessions, however, the girls do not have to sit on their hands. Sometimes, we wish they could sit on their mouths (because of the hemisphere situation)!

At this early age, girls have greater impulse control than boys. The female brain secretes more serotonin which is directly related to impulse control. Girls are more able to monitor and control their behavior than boys—even though, at times, it may not seem like it.

Multitasking

Another area of the brain that develops more rapidly in girls than in boys is the *occipital lobe*. The occipital lobe is the region of the brain that takes in sensory data. Girls can take in more information at one time, whereas boys tend to focus on a singular event. Because of this occipital lobe, girls also have greater differentiation skills, so they can, for instance, tell the difference between mommy's voice and daddy's. They experience and recognize different feelings, such as being able to tell when you are sad or happy. And their senses are able to be more specific—they notice different smells, sounds, and sights before boys are able to.

This greater sensory awareness in girls leads to an ability to handle more information than boys. They are able to register and recognize more incoming information, and to respond accordingly. Girls can be aware of more conversations going on in a room, notice more people who might be in that particular room, and even feel more in response. In essence, this ability is setting the stage for girls to be able to perform multiple tasks at one time. When girls are in middle school, therefore, and need to be aware of all of the social nuances in the cafeteria, their brains are already prepared. Girls in high school can carry on several conversations at once—either in person or on the computer—and, as they become women, girls can discipline their own child, prepare dinner, and plan tomorrow's agenda for work—all at the same time.

Caretaking

Pepper is a dear friend of ours with four adorable children—three boys and one girl. She told us recently about the difference between her daughter, Mary Holland, and her boys. "Mary Holland is my nurturer. She hates it when her big brother is in time-out. She takes him his 'lamby' so he won't be sad. She takes him toys, food, and his sippy cup, and she even tries to stay in time-out with him. His brother Brown, on the other hand, would like for him to be in time-out forever because he gets a turn with the fire truck."

Some of this has to do with Mary Holland's occipital lobe. Although she and Brown are both two, she is able to pick up on the fact that Will is sad more easily than Brown can. She can tell that he is sad and needs to be comforted—or fed, as we girls often think.

Pepper's youngest son, Ian, was born before Mary Holland was two. Pepper also told us that when she would breastfeed Ian, Mary Holland would grab her dolls and hold them up to her chest. Mary Holland has a built-in need to nurture. She wraps her dolls tightly in blankets, feeds them, and cares for them just as her mother cares for Ian. Not only has her mother modeled caretaking behavior, but Mary Holland has an innate sense of nurturing.

Girls' brains secrete more of a hormone called *oxytocin* than boys. *Oxytocin* is directly related to a little girl's and a woman's need to nurture. It is a part of the way God designed Mary Holland for her to cuddle her dolls and comfort her sad brother.

Melissa's sister-in-law, Betsy, recently told us that she tried to raise her girls and boys the same. She didn't want them to have any early gender role stereotypes. So she gave her girls, Mady and Libby, and her boys, John and Sam, all dolls. Guess what happened? Sam and John took the dolls and threw them down. They drove them off cliffs in cars and fought with them. Mady and Libby held and loved their dolls.

Biologically, it makes sense that Mady and Libby would treat their dolls differently than Sam and John. God designed girls and boys to be different. There are, however, girls who lean more toward the boy's side of brain development, as well as boys who lean toward the girl's. This has nothing to do with their sexuality or their future gender roles. It just has to do with the fact that we don't all fit stereotypes and that God designed each of us with a purpose.

EMOTIONAL AND PERSONALITY DEVELOPMENT

We have a twelve-year-old friend named Mamie. She overflows with life. Whatever she does, she does with gusto. When she laughs, she laughs hard. When she rides her bicycle, she likes to be in the front of the pack. When she enjoys a movie, it is the best movie that has ever been made. Mamie also loves to perform. For years, whenever she had a friend spend the night, they would rival any nightclub act in a hairbrush revival of Nat King Cole's "L-O-V-E." When she was a little girl, Mamie's dad gave her the nickname "Soul," which signifies her gusto, her uniqueness, and her personality.

Personality describes what is unique about a girl. Girls develop much of their personality between birth and age five. We're amazed at how many parents say things to us like, "I know my daughter is stubborn. She came out that way," or, "You think she's strong willed as a teenager—you should have seen her stomp when she was two." A great deal of the personality formation of our daughters happens in the Discovery Years. Their sense of determination, exploration, and even their burgeoning sense of self begin to take center stage at this time of their lives.

Three statements, actually commands, are heard most often from the mouths of Discovery-age girls. They are:

- "Pick me up!"
- "Come here!"
- "Watch me!"

Girls not only develop personalities in these first five years, they develop them strongly. That is the job of a toddler. They don't quietly develop—they *loudly* develop. Their needs are not whispered—they are shouted! So let's take a look at the emotional needs behind these three commands.

"Pick Me Up!"—The Need for Affection

Study after study has outlined a baby's profound need for affection. In fact, they don't just need affection, they thrive, physically and emotionally, as a result of the physical care of their primary caregivers. As studies have also shown, babies who are not given this kind of affection are stunted in their development. Both the emotional lives and the future ability to caretake themselves is profoundly affected by the amount of nurturing given these infants.

Toddlers need affection too, but in shorter spurts. "Pick me up" is closely followed by "Put me down!" They need affection but also need to discover their own identities. They still want to be held and cuddled and to crawl up onto your lap and have you read them stories. They still like to be rocked; and they especially crave these things when their newborn sister or brother is receiving this attention. But they also like to be free to wander and explore, especially if their older siblings are doing so.

A dear friend of ours told us that the two sentences she hears most often from her children in the Discovery Years are "I is big!" and "I is your baby!" And she often hears them in the same evening. Her daughter McClain will say, "I is big!" so that she can follow her older brothers and sister out to play or stay up a little later to watch a movie. But without fail, within a few minutes, the late bedtime will catch McClain in her big brown eyes. She will start rubbing them, and wander over to her mom to be picked up.

"I thought you were a big girl and wanted to watch the movie."

"No . . . I is your baby. Pick me up!"

McClain is aware of her need for affection. She is also aware of her need to be a big girl. In the Discovery Years, girls will bounce back and forth between the two. (Remarkably, teenagers behave very similarly.)

Girls from birth to age five will tug on your pant leg to be held and then run from you as fast as their toddling legs will take them. They will wear themselves out and come back to you. These girls need affection. As they grow older, they won't need it (or at least they won't act like they need it) quite as much. But they still do. They need you to hold them, snuggle them, and play with them in ways that involve touch. Touch helps Discovery-age girls know that they are safe and loved.

"Come Here!"—The Need for Interaction

Girls in their Discovery Years are doing just that—discovering. They are fascinated with everything from caterpillars to puppy dogs to other children. They notice a new object and are immediately captivated. What happens next? The girl will wander back to her mother, grab her hand, and start pulling. "Come heew!" "Mommy, Daddy, Grandma, come heew!" Girls from birth to age five discover something they find exciting and immediately want to share. This has to do with the second concept we feel is important in the emotional lives of girls in their Discovery Years—interaction.

Interaction helps a girl learn to socialize in her Discovery Years. As she learns to interact in her primary relationships, she feels more confidence in her interactions with others.

Girls from birth to age five are inviting us to interact constantly. They are inviting us in ways that are loud, entreating, and sound like a broken record, but they are inviting nonetheless. It may be that a girl is inviting her mother to pet a dog with her. She may be inviting her father to play a game or see a spider with her. Regardless of the invitation, these children are experiencing something that they want us to share. Essentially, they are inviting us to interact.

Babies and young girls need interaction for different reasons. A nine-month-old who is not yet saying "Come heew!" is inviting you to respond facially—as she smiles and laughs. When you smile back, she sees that you care about her and that you enjoy her. A two-year-old may need your interaction so that she can assert her independence—she wants to say no but she still needs you to interact, if only to give her the opportunity to say no. A four-year-old needs you to interact to help her learn to relate to others—to share and to be kind.

Last winter we had dinner with our long-time friend Cindy and her daughters, Olivia, age five, and Savannah, age two. After dinner we decided to give them their belated Christmas present, which said in very large words on the box "Assembly Required." We bought them a playhouse that was made up of about fourteen poles, forty-two screws, eighty-four washers, and one fabric tent made to look like a pink cottage with their names on it. This assembly was quite an undertaking.

Five-year-old Olivia really wanted to help. To feel that she was contributing gave her confidence. She was anxious to find the right pole or the right washers. When she handed them to us and was told "Thank you, Olivia" or "Great job!" her eyes lit up with a sense of purpose. Two-year-old Savannah thought she wanted to help. But as Olivia sat beside her and started touching the shiny washers, Savannah changed her mind. For Savannah, we were a backdrop against which she could assert her independence. She wanted to do something different—by herself. She wanted to hold all of the washers and screws—by herself. She would probably have liked to build her own house.

Children in the Discovery Years crave interaction. They want to be a part of whatever you are doing. They want to help—and then, most of the time, they want to do it themselves. But they do want your interaction, though they may want it for different reasons. Our interaction gave Savannah an opportunity to assert her independence and gave Olivia her confidence.

As adults, you have an important role in the interaction of your girls from birth to five. They learn how to relate to the world around them as they learn to relate to you. You are the first to teach them to be kind and to share. You help them develop confidence as you encourage them and give them opportunities to help. As their confidence develops, so does their sense of self, which has much to do with the next command of the Discovery Years: "Watch me!"

"Watch Me!"—The Need to Discover a Sense of Self

A friend of ours told us she used to feel sorry for the small children in her neighborhood park who would shout out "Watch Me!" over and over and over. They would shout it as they reached the top of the slide or reached the top of their arc in the swing. It didn't matter what they were doing—they wanted response and recognition. Our friend said that she worried about these children. "Do they not have anyone paying attention to them at home?" she would wonder. And then her children reached the same age. (If you have a child this age, you're probably snickering.) The kids who are screaming to be watched are being watched all the time.

It doesn't matter how much response they get, they still want more.

This is not because children have an emotional black hole due to a lack of parental love. Nor does it mean they will turn into narcissistic adults (although they will pass through this stage in adolescence). Rather, it means that they are discovering their sense of self.

Once again, girls are developing in the context of relationship. As a girl yells, "Watch me!" from the top of a playground slide, what she is really saying is, "I think I'm doing something great here. Don't you think so?" Girls want to be noticed—to be the object of attention and admiration from the people they love. This helps them discover who they are—their sense of self. For a toddler, those people will be her primary caregivers. As she grows older, she'll try to get the attention of others—teachers, peers, and boys, to name a few. Her way of expressing her need to be noticed will change, also, as she moves away from childhood. Eventually, her makeup, clothes, and activities will all say "watch me" without her ever having to speak the words.

Girls at every age long to be noticed by those most important to them. They want to be the apple of their mother's or father's or aunt's eye. As they shout, "Watch me," from the top of slides, diving boards, and balance beams, they are doing what all toddlers do: they wander away but look back. They want to be free to climb the slide but want you to watch and shout your approval. The wandering has as much to do with her growing sense of self as the approval.

Children in the Discovery Years are beginning (in small toddler-ish ways) to branch out on their own. They are literally crawling and walking away from you. They are climbing and running and jumping and learning to separate themselves from their parents. You want them to do this.

If you overprotect your children and don't allow them to separate, they have trouble developing confidence. They do not believe they are capable if you don't allow them to be capable. They will doubt themselves and their abilities. A little doubt, however, is helpful. You want them to feel confident but not omnipotent. Limitless freedom comes with a price as well. The child who has no boundaries will become too impulsive. She will believe that she can do anything at any time. The answer is in the balance.

Discovery-age girls need your attention. They need you to shout, "That was great!" or, "Good job" from the sidelines of their adventures. They need you to let them go on these adventures so they are able to develop confidence, and then they need you to notice and shout your hearty approval.

What do you want to see in the emotional development of a girl from birth to age five? You want her to feel safe in your care—to feel that she can and will be picked up and cuddled on a regular basis, but also to expect to be put down eventually. You want her to learn to interact, but to interact with kindness. You want her to find her unique personality—her independence, her miniature sense of self, and her will—but she needs to know that your will is stronger than hers. You want her to take initiative and revel in her freedom to go and play, knowing that there are limits that will keep her safe. Finally, you want her to know that you notice her and think she is the best jumper-in-the-water, the best soccer player, the best singer, the best daughter, granddaughter, and girl that God ever made (even if she is third out of five daughters).

SPIRITUAL DEVELOPMENT

These first five years are profoundly important in the spiritual development of girls. They are awakening to this world. How a girl connects with God will be directly related to how she connects in her closest relationships. And she will develop those connections through three important tasks:

- She must learn to trust.
- She must hang on to hope.
- She must dare to imagine.

As she learns to trust, to hope, and to imagine in relationship to those around her, she will develop the capacity to do the same in her relationship with God.

Learning to Trust

Girls in their Discovery Years ask a lot of "whys." They want to know why we say certain things ... why clouds move across the sky ... why fire trucks have sirens. Pretty much anything that can be asked will be asked in the first five years of life. Why? Because girls trust that you know and will provide the answer. Children in these years trust the adults in their lives simply because, in their minds, you are trustworthy. You feed them when they are hungry. You pick them up when they are crying. You change their diapers, take them to the doctor, and provide for all of their basic needs.

The renowned psychologist Erik Erikson believed that a child's ability to trust is directly related to her ability to trust her primary caregivers. If the first people she comes in contact with, most often mom and dad, are consistent—if they offer her stability and ongoing, reliable care, she will learn the concept of trust. She will believe the world is safe, based on the safety of her own home.

On the other hand, if her first world is unsafe—if her parents are abusive or neglectful—she will feel that the rest of the world will be as well. If her primary caregivers are not reliable to provide for her most basic needs, she will inherently believe the same to be true about others. Rather than developing relationships built on trust, hers will be built on mistrust.

Erikson, therefore, believed that the primary task of an infant's caregivers is building trust. Trust creates more trust. As parents, grandparents, or guardians, you are a young girl's first line of defense. She needs to believe deeply that you are trustworthy. Obviously, you won't be able to meet absolutely every need a child has at every moment. Parents need to feed themselves, feel free to go to movies without the child, or both may even require careers outside the home. But every child needs the assurance that her caregivers are trustworthy.

When children are grossly neglected, abandoned, or abused, however, they often don't learn to trust. This crucial developmental characteristic simply doesn't develop in these children. As you can imagine, this profoundly impacts the child's outlook on her parents, her other relationships, her relationship with God, and the world around her.

This often happens with children who were adopted out of abusive or neglectful homes. These children live in a great deal of mistrust. They feel a need to hoard and sometimes steal food, money, and other basic necessities from their adoptive parents. Why? Because these children never learned to trust. They believe they must take care of themselves—even when the evidence points to the contrary.

As trustworthy as the adoptive parents may be, these children never had the opportunity to develop this characteristic that is foundational to their emotional and spiritual lives. This is not to say that the child can't learn to trust. She absolutely can. And we have seen it happen time after time. But trust is not a given the way it is in homes where a child has been cared for and nurtured consistently.

Rachel is an adolescent girl in this very situation. When she was a child, her parents were either drunk or high through most of her first five years. She and her siblings had to fend for themselves. Her older sister remembers searching through dumpsters for food. She doesn't remember much in those years before she and her siblings were removed from the home.

Her only memory of her birth parents is being on a farm. She was a toddler and her father sent the kids to play with horses in the field. As the kids were playing, the horses got spooked. One horse tried to trample Rachel. But, as Rachel tells it, her mom ran under the horse and pulled her out.

This is the only memory Rachel has of her mother. And it is one she clings to with every fiber of her being. In reality, her mother was tragically untrustworthy. She couldn't provide for her children in any way that kept them safe or fed. But this teenage girl clings to the one memory of her mother that demonstrated a shred of care ... of trustworthiness.

As a teenager, Rachel has stolen from her adoptive parents, she has a history of boyfriends who are irresponsible at best, dangerous at worst, and she cannot seem to keep a friend. Rachel's parents are kind, love her deeply, and would do anything to give her the things she missed as a young child. Rachel, however, is desperate to trust. And it is happening—Rachel is slowly learning to trust them, and even more importantly, she is learning to trust God.

Trusting God has been particularly difficult for Rachel. If God allowed her to be in a home like that, how could he be trustworthy? How could he love her and die for her but allow her to be neglected and then removed from her parents? As adults, we understand the concept of free will and sin. We can explain this with a little more rationality. But a teenager has difficulty with this concept. A child doesn't understand.

A girl's spiritual life is deeply affected by her level of trust. If she knows her parents love her and are committed to her good, she will generally believe that she is "lovable" (maybe except in middle school) both by the outside world and by God. Her parents love her. God loves her. Her parents will respond to her needs. So will God. This sounds elementary, but so is the thinking of your daughter in her Discovery Years.

She does not reason in the ways that you do. Her language and comprehension are still very simple. Your tone of voice, facial expression, and body language all communicate more to your daughter at this age than your words.

So, reasoning with your daughter about your trustworthiness is not much of an issue in her Discovery Years. She can't be convinced verbally. What convinces her you are trustworthy is your actions. She knows you are trustworthy by your willingness to pick her up and hug her, take her by the hand and show her that it is okay to touch the dog, and to get on the floor and play dolls with her.

As your daughter learns that you are there and that you are trustworthy, she learns to believe the same is true about others, and then about God. *Trust ripples outward.* As children discover who they are in relationship to their parents, to the adults in their lives, they begin to discover who they are in relationship to God. Trust begets trust. And this kind of trust leads to hope.

Hanging On to Hope

> *Now faith is being sure of what we hope for and certain of what we do not see.*
>
> HEBREWS 11:1
>
> *For in this hope we were saved. But hope that is seen is no hope at all. Who hopes for what he already has? But if we hope for what we do not yet have, we wait for it patiently.*
>
> ROMANS 8:24–25

Trust and hope are foundational to all of our spiritual lives, not just those of girls in the Discovery Years. We trust before we hope. And according to Hebrews, hope leads to faith. Hebrews 11:1 defines faith as "the substance of things hoped for, the evidence of things not seen" (KJV).

In his writings on the development of children, Erik Erikson defines hope as "the belief that even when things are not going well, they will work out in the end." We all need this kind of hope. The Discovery Years are when it begins.

First, your daughter learns to trust you. She knows that she can depend on you to care for her, provide for her, and meet her basic needs. If a two-year-old could verbalize trust, she might say, "My parents take care of me. They feed me, buy me clothes, and carry me when I want to be picked up. They are always there for me."

Hope is taking that trust to the next level. If a two-year-old could verbalize hope, she might say, "My parents will come and pick me up when I fall down and cry." Trust is the belief that you are there. Hope is the belief that you will come soon. In essence, hope is emotional *object permanence.*

Object permanence, which children are developing at this age, is the understanding that something doesn't really disappear even though the child can't see it. If your daughter drops her cookie, it still exists out of her sight. It is on the floor, and Mommy will even stoop to pick it up (which becomes a constant source of fun for little ones!).

Emotional object permanence is the knowledge that, even if what your daughter wants is not there at the moment she wants it, it will come. You will come if she falls down. You will give her a cookie "in a minute." She can go outside as soon as she picks up her toys.

Hope is waiting with the expectation that the one we trust is going to come through for us. The development of this kind of hope is a positive sign in girls. When a child isn't overly upset (please hear the "overly") about having to wait for a cookie or to go outside—when the gratification of her needs isn't immediate and she doesn't have a complete meltdown—she is learning the concept of hope.

As with trust, this kind of hope leads to much bigger hopes. Learning to wait expectantly for a cookie at age five teaches her a basic understanding of hope. With this understanding, waiting for a "best friend" at twelve or a boyfriend at nineteen is not nearly as difficult. And at thirty, the waiting expectantly to become pregnant is not entirely foreign. It can still be painfully difficult to hope in certain circumstances. But the child who has learned to hope in the Discovery Years has a more foundational understanding of hope that she can draw on. Again, smaller hopes translate to larger hopes and involve the developing of her little spirit.

First, your daughter learns to believe that you are trustworthy. "If mom says she is coming, she is coming." This trust transforms into hope as the child learns to wait. "Mom may not be coming this second, but I know she is coming because what she says is true." You teach your daughter to hope as you teach her that, even if your response is delayed, you will come through for her. And you do so by being a consistent, supportive presence in her life.

Hope, or the lack thereof, moves outward, as does trust. Your daughter learns to trust and hope at home first. And then the hope ripples over into her picture of God. Listen to how the answers of one precocious five-year-old demonstrate the rippling effect of trust and hope.

When have you felt closest to God?

"When I'm snuggling with Mommy and Daddy."

What is most important to you?

"Mommy, I mean God."

If you could ask God anything, what would you ask him?

"Would you please make Mommy never spank me again?"

Do you believe a relationship with God is important? If yes, why? And if no, why not?

"Yes, because I love God—and that's not a girly question."

It is obvious that this little girl feels connected to her parents. She trusts them. She also trusts God. She believes that he could keep her mommy from ever spanking her again (although we know he doesn't work quite that way). And if she asks, she has hope that he will. Her parents are trustworthy, as is God. They come through for her, as will he. The trust and hope are inextricably linked, and it is her imagination that helps her return to trust and hope when things become difficult.

Dare to Imagine

Children in the Discovery Years naturally possess an imagination. They fully believe in all things believable and unbelievable that you tell them. This has to do with their innate sense of trust. If you tell your daughter at three that she is beautiful, then she believes she is beautiful. If you say you are driving to the grocery store, she doesn't suspect that you are going to trick her and take her to the doctor instead. If you say Santa Claus is real, then Santa Claus is real and her eyes twinkle while waiting expectantly for him.

As you help your daughter develop trust and hope during these years, you also help develop her imagination. And her imagination has as much to do with the development of her spirit as do trust and hope.

In her book *A Tree Grows in Brooklyn*, Betty Smith gives a poignant explanation for the necessity of imagination in a child's life. In this conversation, a grandmother-to-be is telling her daughter of the power of stories. She talks about the importance of sharing the Bible, Shakespeare, and Santa Claus with her baby girl. When asked why, this was the grandmother's response:

> "Because," explained Mary Rommely simply, "the child must have a valuable thing which is called imagination. The child must have a secret world in which live things that never were. It is necessary that she believe. She must start out by believing in things not of this world. Then when the world becomes too ugly for living in, the child can reach back and live in her imagination. I, myself, even in this day and at my age have great need of recalling the miraculous lives of the saints and the great miracles that have come to pass on earth. Only by having these things in my mind can I live beyond what I have to live for."

The imagination is what enables the trust and hope to continue when life becomes painful. Girls need to hear stories, to be read books, and to play games that foster their imaginations. To hear the story of the little boy's room that transforms into a jungle in *Where The Wild Things Are* or to believe that her daddy really is a terrible giant that is trying to eat her will cause her imagination to stretch. Jonah and the Whale, Daniel in the Lions' Den, and other Bible stories also can stir her imagination to see life beyond her own.

As a girl hears about God and Jesus, her imagination will provide her with an anchor. She will have tools to move past the four walls of her everyday life, past the tragedy of the particular moment and back into truth. When her feelings are hurt, she can fall back on stories from the Bible and on God's profound love for her. Imagination is the soil in which these spiritual truths take root. What you teach your daughter in the Discovery Years as well as who you are in relationship to her helps to foster the growth of her imagination, trust, and hope.

PARENTING DURING THE DISCOVERY YEARS

As you watch your daughter wake up, your job is relatively simple. You sing to her, pray with her, snuggle with her, and teach her about Jesus. You create space for her to grow, but stay near enough to cuddle. You allow her to toddle down the lane, but only within the sound of your shouts of admiration and delight.

Sounds simple, doesn't it? We know it's not. We know that many of you with daughters in the Discovery Years feel much like Anne Lamott, in her book *Operating Instructions*:

> There are a couple of things I want to remember about Sam's earlier days, his youth, now that he's kind of an old guy with no umbilical cord. The first thing happened the day my

friend Peg and I brought him home from the hospital, during what for me felt like the most harrowing ride a person could take through San Francisco. The first time we hit a pothole, I thought, "Well, that's that, his neck just snapped; we broke him. He's a quadriplegic now. But we did get him home safely....

You may have felt the same fears on your baby girl's ride home from the hospital ... or during her first bath ... or the first time you watched her big brother swing her over his head. Parenting is a terrifying, wonderful job. And every age has its parts that are terrifying and its parts that are wonderful.

CHAPTER 3

The Adventurous Years: Six to Eleven

I would be starting to school in a week. I never looked forward more to anything in my life. Hours of wintertime had found me in the tree house, looking over at the schoolyard, spying on multitudes of children through a two-power telescope Jem had given me, learning their games, following Jem's red jacket through wriggling circles of blind man's bluff, secretly sharing their misfortunes and minor victories. I longed to join them.

HARPER LEE, *TO KILL A MOCKINGBIRD*

As a young girl, I (Melissa) longed to be Queen of the Merry-Go-Round. The merry-go-round was the focus of all energy and powermongering of the children at AB Austin Elementary School. Each day at recess they started the merry-go-round spinning, and everyone who dared pushed and shoved their way to the center. Only an elect few were able to make it. Whoever did gained the unofficial, widely revered title of King or Queen of the Merry-Go-Round.

Like Scout in *To Kill a Mockingbird*, I longed to join them. One day, I finally decided it was time for me to claim my throne. The merry-go-round started spinning and I hopped on. I pulled myself with the bars, tried to nicely throw the other children off, and finally reached the pinnacle of my hopes—the center. I sat there for a few moments of glory, watching the disappointed faces whirl around me. As the whirling continued, however, something tragic happened. My dress was somehow caught in the spinning gears. It no longer participated in the spinning, while I did. What that meant was that my dress started wrapping itself around me ... tighter and tighter and tighter. The merry-go-round could not stop fast enough, and my reign ended as quickly as it began—with my lunch coming up all over my beautiful dress that my grandmother and aunt had made for me. My dress had to be cut and I was escorted off my momentary throne.

It is easy to hear that story and to shudder in sympathy with my humiliation. My memory of that day, however, is one without shame. It was more of an adventure than an embarrassment.

My willingness to go after the throne and my lack of self-consciousness about the outcome are representative of girls in their Adventurous Years. Girls age six to eleven are freer, with fewer limitations. They don't feel as much of the self-consciousness that haunts girls throughout adolescence, and they rebound from their hurts much faster than those in the Narcissistic Years. Your daughter comes home from school complaining that her best friend played with someone else at recess. You sit down to listen as she talks and spills tears all over the kitchen table. And just as you are getting up to call this friend's mom to tell her how terribly her daughter hurt your daughter, she is on her way out the door to play kick-the-can with her neighborhood buddies.

The adventurousness of girls is a relative term, however. Growing up, Melissa was on the wild side of adventurous, while Sissy was more on the sweet side. Melissa chased boys, picked neighbors' flowers, and climbed in and out of windows. She always gathered the neighborhood kids together to tell them what their next escapade would be. Melissa's life in her Discovery Years would make a great coming-of-age movie.

Sissy was a much quieter six- to eleven-year-old. Sissy liked to milder adventures. She took gymnastics and dance lessons and loved to ride bikes with Ryan and Blair, her best "boy" friends. But she would have watched the merry-go-round from a distance and wouldn't have climbed in or out of a window to save her life. She stretched herself by reading and learning. She liked to play games and sports that didn't require daring and didn't draw that amount of attention.

It is important to realize girls age six to eleven are different. They all are adventurous, but that adventurousness comes out in various ways. Some are quieter than others, but the freedom of this time is still there.

PHYSICAL DEVELOPMENT

Girls in their Adventurous Years are dependent on their bodies. Those bodies are helping them learn to kick a soccer ball, turn a cartwheel, and pedal a bike. They are spurring on their adventurousness. Within and without, your daughter's body is going through a period of slow, consistent growth during these years. Her squishy, chubby, adorable toddler body is making the gradual, long shift to the awkwardness of early adolescence. This affects her motor development, her memory, her emotions, and her femininity.

Motor Development

From six to eleven, girls are growing at an average of two to three inches per year. This is not lightning fast in terms of growth, but it is significant. Their muscles are, thankfully, growing right along with their bodies, and this muscle growth enables girls to use more of the gross motor skills that were lacking in the Discovery Years.

For a four-year-old to play tennis would be difficult. She can pick up balls and roll them. She could even throw them to her dad. But she would most likely not have the hand-eye coordination to hit a ball with a racket—nor would she have the strength. Eight-year-olds, however, can and do.

As we said before, these are the years of tennis lessons, gymnastics, soccer practice, and basketball. These are the years of dads running alongside their daughters' bikes as the training wheels come off. Girls are not only able but need to participate in activities to develop these gross motor skills. This helps to increase both their competence at various activities and their confidence in themselves.

Memory

A conversation with a nine-year-old often isn't much of a conversation. It is more like a soliloquy. The following is a typical car ride home for a mother and her nine-year-old daughter:

> "Hi, Mom."
>
> "Hi, honey, how was school?"
>
> "Well, Johnny didn't do his homework *again*. The teacher told him, in front of all of us, that if he didn't bring his homework tomorrow he'd have to pull a card. Do you know what it means, to pull a card? It means he won't be able to go out for recess the next day. I'm glad I've never had to pull a card. Would you and Dad be mad if I did? It seems like girls don't really pull cards as much as boys do. But did you know that Caitlin pulled a card last week? It was because she was talking to Chelsea. They were talking about a birthday party they went to on Friday night. They get in trouble for that sometimes. I'm glad I don't get in trouble much. Are you mad because I forgot to clean up the brownies yesterday? I didn't mean to, and I promise I will help you clean up the kitchen today."

The soliloquy has to do with the brain development of girls in their Adventurous Years. By and large, their brains are mostly formed at this time. Girls' brains, however, look very different from boys' at this age. The predominant difference is in the area of the brain called the *hippocampus*, which is much larger in girls. The hippocampus controls memory ability and functioning. Because of the size of their hippocampus, girls can and often do remember every detail of their day. They remember things you often wish they'd forget, or at least maybe remember with a little more brevity.

Emotions and the Limbic System

Toddlers throw temper tantrums quite regularly. When a three-year-old can't wrestle the toy she wants away from her brother, she has a fit. In some ways, this is out of her control. Her brain is not yet developed in a way that enables her to regulate her emotions.

When she is eight, however, it is a different story. Not that eight-year-olds don't have temper tantrums—they most certainly do. But your eight-year-old daughter does have the capacity to control her emotions. The limbic system in her brain is much more developed than it was in her Discovery Years. This portion of her brain regulates sensory information and emotions. She is able to take in more information and categorize it.

Femininity

Because of Winn-Dixie, *My Girl*, *Madeleine*, *To Kill a Mockingbird*, *Little House on the Prairie*—all of these books and movies are centered around girls in their Adventurous Years. And these girls are adventurous. They are not solely inside playing with dolls, although they also do that. They are riding bikes, climbing trees, hunting for mysterious creatures like Boo Radley, and doing their best to save their friends (who are often dogs).

Hormones are just beginning to enter the brains of girls in their Adventurous Years. In today's society, girls as young as eight are starting their periods, though this is not the norm. But the girls who do begin menstruation early will move more quickly into the next stage of development.

While boys in their six-to-eleven years are becoming more masculine, girls typically don't begin the journey into traditional femininity until the next stage. They are just as happy to play in the creek as they are to play with their dollhouse. And they do both. If a girl is going to be a tomboy, she is at the full stature of tomboyishness in her years from six to eleven. She will often wear bows in her hair as she fishes in the creek.

Melissa's mom, Margaret, told us about her group during her Adventurous Years, the "Trespassing Busters." She and her neighborhood girlfriends (many of whom included her five sisters) loved to play on the train trestles. They would wait for the trains to blow their horns, and then run down the trestle. They would also go inside the root cellar under the house and shout out every curse word they had ever heard, none of which were ever allowed in their strict home.

Margaret is one of the most feminine women we know. But she has also hung on to a bit of the adventurousness of her six-to-eleven years. And that would be our hope for all Adventurous-age girls. We hope that, as they trade climbing trees for catching boys, they will not completely leave behind the wildness and the sweetness of these years.

EMOTIONS AND PERSONALITY DEVELOPMENT

Emotionally, these are unfettered years for girls. They are free to go, play, do, try, risk—without much concern about what others are thinking. These are years that are significant for working through fears, developing confidence, gaining social skills, and discovering their individual personalities. In many ways, girls in the Adventurous Years find their uniqueness with both courage and creativity.

In the last chapter, we talked about the emotional development of Discovery-age girls in commands such as "Pick me up," and "Watch me!" In this chapter, we talk about development with questions.

- "Mom, would you leave the light on?"
- "Do I have to practice?"
- "Can I have a friend over?"
- "How do I make them like me?"

Girls from six to eleven years are curious seekers—for all kinds of information. They are not as much about edicts as they are about questions. So we start with a question that echoes down the halls of homes everywhere.

"Mom, Would You Leave the Light On?" —Dealing with Fear

Children from six to eleven are undoubtedly adventurous. But often the adventure ends at night. When the lights go out, their fears come to life. It may be fantastical fears such as monsters under the bed and witches in the closet to more realistic fears such as failing a test or losing a parent to death. These fears often keep them from going to sleep and keep many children at this age from spending the night out.

Now I lay me down to sleep,
I pray the Lord my soul to keep.
If I should die before I wake,
I pray the Lord my soul to take.

This prayer is probably the most common bedtime prayer in this country. For a child in her Discovery Years, the repetition and sing-songiness of this prayer is comforting. The words of this prayer, however, can be frightening for a child in her Adventurous Years. We actually toyed with the idea of calling this age the Literal Years in a girl's life because of their concrete thinking. This prayer, taken literally, is alarming. It speaks directly to the fear of death that so many girls have from age six to eleven.

It is easy to understand why girls at this age struggle with fear. The imaginations of the younger Adventurous-age girls are still in full swing, so they really do believe in the possibilities of monsters and witches. The older girls may have confidence during the day that no such thing exists; but in the darkness of night, they wonder. On the other hand, girls at this age are beginning to be aware of the realities of life. They know that their uncle with cancer is going to die soon. They heard that their neighbors were robbed. They actually overheard the news story about a child who was kidnapped.

Girls at this age are literal thinkers. This can play to their fears—but it can also play against them. Their trust in the adults in their life and their growing trust in God as their Father is what makes the difference.

The children's series *Veggie Tales* has tapped into this idea and has come up with a memorable song called "God Is Bigger Than the Boogeyman." The kids in our second-through-fourth-grade camp sing this song incessantly. We're glad. We believe they desperately need to hear the message, which is likely why they have latched onto it. Girls in their Adventurous Years need to know they are safe, and they need to know that there is someone bigger than they are who loves them and is protecting them.

How do you teach this important truth? You teach it verbally as you live it out yourselves. Parents who are terribly fearful often raise fearful children. Even without parental influence, fear can be debilitating for girls in this age. We do, however, know the truth. God is bigger than the boogeyman, after all.

"Do I *Have* to Practice?": Learning New Skills

The years from six to eleven are the years in which girls begin to learn music, singing, drawing, dancing, languages—but they also learn other activities such as soccer, gymnastics, basketball, and cheerleading.

We have said these could be considered the Adventurous or the Literal Years, but they could also be considered the Busy Years. It is difficult for girls at this age to schedule counseling appointments in our offices between soccer and basketball practices, piano lessons, and horseback riding. But these are significant ways that Adventurous-age girls develop their personalities.

It is in these years that girls begin to excel in certain areas. Psychologist Erik Erikson calls these the years of "Industry vs. Inferiority." *Industry* has to do with the competence in different activities girls develop in their Adventurous Years. Girls at this age learn various skills—skills that you, many times, have to push them to become involved in.

What does this industry develop in girls? Why should you push them to try different activities? Pushing is definitely one of the least enjoyable aspects of parenting six-to-eleven-year-olds. It is important, however, because these activities help them develop confidence, teach them to fail and succeed, and introduce them to the concepts of working with others.

How do you help your daughter develop confidence? Girls develop confidence as they discover that they are able—able to learn the positions in ballet, paint an actual painting, dribble a soccer ball, work with other girls to score a basketball goal. As a parent, you want to give your daughter opportunities to feel able and competent. It can even help to focus that competence in one area.

Psychologist and author Mary Pipher talks about the need for girls to have a "North Star," an activity that they attach to that guides them through many of the bumps they will go through in their Adventurous Years. This activity becomes her "thing"—an activity she does regularly and that she is known for by other children. For some girls, it is dance, for others, horseback riding, sports, reading, music. It doesn't really matter what her thing is—she just needs one. The activity will most likely change as she grows older. But it definitely helps when she feels awkward in gym class to know that she has horseback riding to look forward to that weekend.

Girls need to feel successful in something ... whether that is an activity or a relationship. Some girls may not be gifted athletically or artistically, but they are great with younger children. These girls would feel competence and even success volunteering with underprivileged kids.

At this age it can be harmful, however, to push a girl too much toward one thing. If she only has one activity, it starts to define who she is. For example, her soccer performance from a previous game could dictate how she feels about herself for the entire week. She needs other activities—other outlets in which to feel success.

On the other side of success is, as we know, failure. Kids, however, don't know this—until they learn. And the learning process is painful, sometimes as much for parents as it is for children.

We talk often at Daystar about how, in our culture, we teach children to succeed but not to fail. I (Sissy) recently had a thirteen-year-old in counseling for an eating disorder. She barely ate a meal a day, and the meal consisted mostly of apples and cereal. This young woman was deeply perfectionistic. She was bright, strong, capable, and courageous. But she had stopped eating. And no amount of success in any area of her life was going to make her start again.

I brought her single mother in for a counseling session. I had a conversation with her that I have with many parents of girls with eating disorders.

"I'm afraid Caroline is almost too successful. She expects perfection from everything she does. She actually achieves it most of the time. She does fail, however. And she has no idea what to do when she does not meet her own or others' expectations. One of the things I would like to see happen is for her to be able to accept her failures. This is a place you could really help your daughter.

I want you to talk to her about your own failures. Tell her at the dinner table when you made a silly mistake at work. Casually mention that you hurt the feelings of one of your friends."

As I said these words to this distraught mother, her eyes glazed over. She said, "I'm not really sure what you mean. Caroline does very well. I don't know how I can help with that."

Her mother was not comfortable with her own failure and was modeling that for Caroline.

We teach children how to succeed but not to fail—often by example. Unless taught differently, girls will believe their acceptance is based on their performance. When they accept their failure and feel loved in spite of that failure, their acceptance will be based on something deeper. Failure is a means by which they—and we, as adults—discover more about grace.

How do you help your child live through her failures? As we said, talk about your own. Live in a household that models forgiveness for mistakes, whether the error is spilled milk or a misplaced phone message. And finally, don't treat failure as a taboo subject. Don't ignore the missed basket in basketball. Talk about it. Ask her if she could have done anything different. And then move on. Take her to get ice cream after her failures and successes. Help her lighten up and see that there is much about her that is good and enjoyable *even when she makes mistakes.*

Failures and successes are a huge part of the benefits of the various and sundry activities of the Discovery Years. But what is probably the biggest benefit of these activities for girls? And where do they develop the most confidence? You guessed it—relationships.

"Can I Have a Friend Over?"—Developing Friendships

Ages six to eleven are years of birthday parties and sleepovers. Girls are learning not only more of who they want to be but who they want their friends to be as well.

In the earlier grades of this age bracket, birthday parties are often made up of an entire class. As girls grow older, however, they start to experiment with different groups. These are not the exclusive cliques that develop in middle school. These are girls trying out different friends to see where and with whom they might connect.

Parents will, however, watch at every age as girls are left out. We talk more about this in the next chapter. But the fact of the matter is that girls can be, and too often are, ruthless. As they get closer to middle school, this ruthlessness nears its pinnacle. No matter what you do to prevent it and how deeply you dread it, your daughter will feel left out at some point as she moves into her preteen and teenage years. Unfortunately, some girls are left out more than others—often with no explanation.

One of these girls comes to counseling at Daystar. Her name is Betsy, and she is engaging, warm, and very kind. Her mother brought her in because she was becoming more and more anxious about her schoolwork.

During a meeting, I (Sissy) had Betsy draw on two different sheets of paper. On one paper, I asked her to draw things that the other children knew about her at school. On the other, she drew the things the kids at school didn't know about her.

These were her words: "Well, first of all they don't know that I worry most of the time. They think I'm just shy, but I'm really worried about a lot of things. That's why I don't talk very much. They also don't know that I like to look for geodes. Geodes are these really cool rocks with crystals inside them. Let me see ... oh, they don't know that I like to watch *Little House on the Prairie.* I can't think of anything else. Is that enough?" (She was drawing silently for a few minutes.) "Oh ... I thought of one more thing. They don't know that I need a really good friend."

These words could reduce any parent to tears in a moment, and definitely did me. Betsy doesn't feel like she has any friends at school. She says the kids ignore her or give her "really weird looks." It doesn't make sense.

How can you help your daughter when she comes home with Betsy's story? You know it's going to happen. You can't prevent it. But how can you respond? We answer these questions and more in chapter 9, where we look more closely at the relational world of girls.

We will say, however, that girls in this age often don't say when their feelings are hurt. They may feel awkward or afraid. They may not even understand what is happening. But girls in their Adventurous Years often have physical symptoms of internal problems. If your daughter has a stomachache every day when you pick her up from school, if she starts to have headaches when she is supposed to play with certain friends, or if she stops eating the lunch you send with her, start asking questions.

You may also find that things seem okay during the day, but she no longer wants to sleep by herself. This could be one of those physical symptoms. Dig a little deeper into these things. Talk with her. Draw her out verbally, even though she may have trouble finding the exact words to describe what is happening.

Bedtime is a great time to talk about difficult things. Because they are tired, girls are often more vulnerable at night. This is an easy time to ask questions about how things are going at school.

Life for your daughter changes drastically as she enters school. She is thrown into an entirely new world. She has teachers to please, boys to run from, and girls to befriend. In reality, that's a lot of pressure for a six- to eleven-year-old. She needs you, as her parent, to be a strong, safe place where she can run to when things get hard. She needs you to ask and to listen. She needs you to hug her, enjoy her, and help her see that you know, even when her peers don't, the truth of who she really is. You know she likes geodes and *Little House on the Prairie*. And most importantly, you know she is a delightful, unique, extraordinary individual who any girl in school would be lucky to have as a friend.

How Do I Make Them Like Me?: Choosing a Relational Strategy

The social pressure rises exponentially as girls enter grade school. As they become older, they experience more of both a desire to be liked and a need to connect. Because other girls can be and often are ruthless, this can become a problem.

All of us, at some time in our lives, choose a particular relational strategy. Many of these strategies find their beginnings in the six-to-eleven-year-old age bracket. A strategy is a style of relating—a self we become that we think people will like.

For example, consider one little girl who has a strong desire to please her first grade teacher. She sits still in her desk. She makes sure she learns all her spelling words. And she uses all the manners she learned at home. Soon, this young lady becomes the unofficial favorite of her teacher, and she is allowed a few extra privileges, definitely winning extra smiles and attention. The extra smiles and attention, however, only reinforce her theory: "If I am good, then I will be liked." See the strategy? It often lasts well into adulthood and turns into a perfectionist who is driven to please and perform for those around her.

Or consider another girl in first grade who desperately wants to be liked by her peers. She is naturally funny and gets a great response from the other children in her class by making jokes. While they laugh, however, the teacher frowns. This little girl is sent to the coatroom on an almost daily basis. These are the words of this little girl (who is now an adult): "I never even thought about pleasing my teacher. All I could think was how do I get through a day without being sent to the coatroom and what can I do to cover up the fact that I don't have any idea what I'm doing?"

Do you see her strategy? She covers up her academic insecurities by making others laugh. This little girl becomes the class clown.

Both the perfectionist and the class clown survived their elementary, middle, and high school years. They are, in fact, the authors of this book. It is easy for us to look back on our own Adventurous Years and see the beginnings of the formation of our personalities. I (Sissy) still struggle with perfectionism on a daily basis, and I (Melissa) am still trying to stay out of the coatroom!

So what do you do with your perfectionistic or coatroom daughter? You definitely can't change her style of relating. What you can do, however, is help round out her strategies. You can help children like Sissy see that it is okay to fail—that her performance is not what garners her love or acceptance by others. You can help children like Melissa see that they have things to offer besides their wit. As she enters school and a new relational world, your daughter will develop strategies, but you can help her know that there is more to her than just those strategies.

God is growing your daughter into the woman he has created her to be. He is developing her personality—through her social world, through her successes and failures, and even through her fears. God is using all of these things to help her find and use the ways he has uniquely gifted your daughter.

SPIRITUAL DEVELOPMENT

Children in their Adventurous Years love to talk and think about God. They have wonderful questions and are hungry to hear the answers. We define *spirit* as the part of a girl that is aware of and responsive to God. Children from six to eleven are both, in ample measure.

We asked girls in the Adventurous Years what they would ask God if they could ask anything. These are just a few of their questions:

> *"Why do you love me so much that you would die for me?"*

> *"What is it like in heaven? Will my dog Otis get to go? And can I have my own room?"*

"Could you make it where nobody will ever be hurt or sick again?"

"Would you get my parents back together and stop them from fighting?"

"Why did Grandpa die?"

"Would you take away my scary thoughts?"

"Could you make the boys be nice to the girls for one day?"

What do you hear in the questions of these girls? Pets, death, heaven, and taking away things that are painful are the themes that run throughout the questions. There is also a great deal of honesty. These girls are not afraid to ask about things they don't understand ("Why did Grandpa have to die?"). They are not afraid to ask for things that are huge ("Could you make it where nobody will ever be hurt or sick again?") or relatively insignificant ("Could you make the boys be nice?"). Much of this is, again, because they are freer in these six-to-eleven years.

The adventurousness of girls in these years spills over into their relationships with God. As we have talked about since the introduction, the identities of girls are found in the context of relationship. From six to eleven years of age, their relationship with God is one that is becoming more significant and more of a necessity in their lives. They want something and they ask him for it. If something is confusing—they'll ask. If something is painful—they just ask him to take it away. These are the voices of young people who are aware of and responsive to God, and it is this very awareness and responsiveness that Jesus talks about in the Bible.

Awareness

At that time Jesus, full of joy through the Holy Spirit said, "I praise you, Father, Lord of heaven and earth, because you have hidden these things from the wise and learned, and revealed them to little children."

LUKE 10:21

The little children Jesus spoke of in this verse were aware of things that adults weren't—wise and learned adults even. They will lose this awareness soon, but for now, in the Adventurous Years, girls are aware of and responsive to God in ways that make them very perceptive. Listen to the words of several parents of six- to eleven-year-old girls.

"Our daughter has a sweet spirit and is very loving and kind. She is always thinking of others. We had a dear friend whose husband died and Casey wrote the woman a beautiful note we didn't even know about, until the woman called to share what it meant to her."

"Once when she was in first grade, she and her twin brother asked to bring home a handicapped boy to play. As my son rolled dice for him, Drew fed him a popsicle and wiped his face."

"I remember when she was eight or nine and at soccer practice. There was one little girl whose feelings had gotten hurt and had run over to the corner where no one could see her. Becca noticed, though, and went over to that girl, talked to her, consoled her, and then got the girl to come back and join the others. Her perceptive abilities of how people feel is one that we believe flows from her faith and love that God has given her."

The perceptive abilities of these girls have to do with the awareness that God has placed inside them during these years. *It is intuitiveness in its beginning stages.* This is what we believe Jesus was talking about in Luke. God reveals these things to the little children. He gives them an awareness of the world around them and of himself, an awareness that is part of what leads to the childlike faith that is talked about in Scripture.

In the Adventurous Years, girls develop new levels of awareness. They are aware of others around them who hurt and are in need. They have learned to trust, and, as we mentioned in the last chapter, trust ripples outward. In their Adventurous Years, girls develop a foundational trust and understanding of God that comes with their awareness.

Responsiveness

> *At that time the disciples came to Jesus and asked, "Who is the greatest in the kingdom of heaven?" He called a little child and had him stand among them. And he said: "I tell you the truth, unless you change and become like little children, you will never enter the kingdom of heaven. Therefore, whoever humbles himself like this child is the greatest in the kingdom of heaven."*
>
> MATTHEW 18:1–4

What did the child in this verse do that led Jesus to believe that he was humble? As far as we know, the child didn't speak a word. "He called a little child and had him stand among them." Jesus called this child and he came. He responded. That is the way of children. One of the predominant and most enjoyable characteristics of children from age six to eleven is their responsiveness. It is also one of the most spiritual.

Again, in contrast to teenagers, the responsiveness of children is refreshing. In our groups at Daystar, we have to teach teenage girls to respond to each other. Children do it naturally.

When Kathleen, my (Sissy's) sister, was six years old, our parents divorced. The actual day that it happened, Kathleen had her best friend, Lila, over to play. Our mom thought Lila might help Kathleen get her mind off what had happened. What Lila did, however, was the exact opposite.

I was drying my hair in my bathroom, which was across the hall from Kathleen's room. The girls were in there with the door shut, playing—or so I thought. A few minutes after they had gone inside, I heard a loud sound. I turned off my hairdryer and went to the door to investigate. Loudly enough to be heard through the door, Lila was wailing. "No, Kathleen, this just can't happen. This is the worst thing I've ever heard. Your parents can't divorce. What are we going to do?"

With all of the awareness and humility of a child, Lila responded. She cried with Kathleen and said the words Kathleen was feeling inside. Jesus could have been saying, "Be like this child Lila." Teenagers and adults lose their responsiveness in the mire of self-consciousness or being afraid they might not respond "the right way." Children just respond.

They have the same kind of response to God. Jesus calls, and they come. At camps we give our kids an opportunity to accept Christ. In the middle and high school camps, the kids often watch each other to see whose hands go up. The second through fourth graders don't care. Their hands shoot up without hesitation—often every hand in the room. These children don't care what the others around them are doing, or even if they've accepted Christ before. They want to again. It is their nature to respond.

For girls, the response is largely relational. Boys in this age bracket respond to challenges and to dares. They light fires, climb buildings, and even stick their tongues to icy flagpoles to prove their "manhood" to their friends (if you've seen *A Christmas Story*, you get the image).

Girls, however, respond to relationships. It may be their relationship with you, with their friends, or with God, but they respond in the context of relationship.

The little girl playing soccer responded when she saw that her teammate was hurt. The girl who wrote the note responded to her mom's friend when she knew that she was sad. The girl who gave the popsicle to the handicapped boy knew he needed help.

Like the story in Matthew, these girls were called and they came. It wasn't literally Jesus calling, but they were responding to a part of who God had created each of these girls to be. He called and, out of the awareness and responsiveness that floods through their Adventurous Years, they came. Sounds simple, doesn't it?

Simplicity

> *When I was a child, I talked like a child, I thought like a child, I reasoned like a child. When I become a man, I put childish ways behind me.*
>
> 1 Corinthians 13:11

What does it mean to talk, think, and reason like a child? We have already said that children are aware and responsive, which we believe Jesus calls us all to be, but they are also simple. They learn and respond to simplicity.

Our friend who teaches a catechism class to fourth graders taught the same class to a group of high school students several years ago. We got to come and watch. These teenagers took the simple truths the fourth graders accepted at face value and dissected them bit by bit under the wise guidance of our friend, Russ. It is definitely a good thing for teenagers to dissect and discover truth on their own, but it is a tremendous gift of the Adventurous Years that children accept simple truth at face value.

The thinking of girls from six to eleven years is simple and concrete. It is black-and-white. They are literal, thinking in terms of right and wrong—good and bad. For them, things are exactly as they are presented. There are no underlying motives or hidden agendas. They believe what you tell them and are hungry to be told. Your teaching with this age bracket needs to fall in line with their way of thinking.

Several summers ago, I (Melissa) got a new toilet at the lake house where we have camp. This toilet serves all the boys who come to our camps—often eighteen at once. As you can imagine, normal toilets don't last long under this kind of pressure. So I had to go another route. I bought instead what is called a Powerflush, which is a toilet that sounds a lot like an airplane taking off. It was installed during second-through-fourth-grade camp, much to the delight of the kids. In those first few days, more boys (and girls) went to the bathroom than I ever remember in a forty-eight-hour time period. They were fascinated.

I saw it as a teaching opportunity. At Daystar we try to take ordinary things—that kids think about and are interested in—and use them as teaching tools. I have taught over the years on everything from rocks to pancakes to the love of puppy dogs. At this camp, though, we talked about the Powerflush.

I had the kids describe what happens in the process of the Powerflush (which they did in a little more detail than I might have preferred). After several of them answered, I asked "Do any of you ever feel like you need a Powerflush in your life?" I talked about how we all have things that are yucky from time to time inside us—jealousy, anger, meanness. In those times, we need a Powerflush. And the spirit of God is who does the flushing. As I asked the question again, "Who feels like they need a Powerflush?" hands shot up all over the room. These second through fourth graders got it. And the Powerflush became our theme for the rest of the week. They would go back to that concept again and again. After a little girl yelled at a boy for taking her fishing pole, for instance, she would say, "I need a Powerflush." After a little boy tried to cut the dinner line, he would say, "I need a Powerflush." In many ways, that was the most honest talk I have ever had with second through fourth graders on the subject of sin.

These kids understood—and they understood quickly that they needed cleansing from their sin. They were aware and responsive, and the simplicity of a toilet grabbed their attention.

Jesus calls us over and over to be like children. Much of the reason can be seen in the girls of the Adventurous Years. They are not complicated; they are wild, free, sweet, and spontaneous; they are humble in their awareness of others; they hunger, search, and long for truth; and when they find that truth, they respond.

It is our job, as adults, to give these girls opportunities to respond. Sunday school, vacation Bible school, family devotionals, camps as they get older—all of these are places where girls can seek and find God in their simplicity.

Someone suggested recently that if your daughter had to be stuck somewhere in her development, you would want her to be stuck in her Adventurous Years. Of course, no one wants their daughter to get stuck, but you do want to enjoy her in this age (even as you enjoy her at every age). You want to help her learn with awareness, simplicity, and responsiveness who God is creating her to be.

PARENTING DURING THE ADVENTUROUS YEARS

I (Melissa) remember my tenth birthday. I really wanted a blue-eyed, curly headed doll. I also wanted a shiny silver pistol. My parents gave me both. I remember standing in front of my birthday cake holding one in each hand for the picture and feeling sad. Somehow, I knew it was probably my last year to receive a doll or a gun.

Six- to eleven-year-old girls believe they are cowboys and nurturing mothers at the same time. These are the years of adventure—of learning more about who they are as they enter the world of school, and who they would like to be as they grow in their awareness of others. They are years that are tender and hopeful and fun, both for girls and for you as a parent.

But they trade in their guns and dolls as they move into middle school. The guns become sassy back-talk and the dolls become their cell phones that are glued to their ears in the Narcissistic Years.

As parents, you have a unique opportunity in these years of adventure. Your daughter is asking questions and looking to you for the answers. In the next stage of her life, as a teenager, she will often look to outside influences such as peers and other adults for those answers. But for now, you are her homeroom teacher whom she looks up to and wants to please.

These years are adventurous, and her adventurousness may take her into a few areas you might not really like to see her go: lying ("I already did my homework"), stealing (such as a pack of gum from the grocery), and whining (manipulation in its earliest forms) are a few of the most common issues for parents of Adventurous-age girls.

But again, her thinking is concrete. As her homeroom teacher, you have an opportunity to give her responses that speak to that concrete thinking. Many adolescents who struggle with lying say that they started getting away with it in these six-to-eleven years. Consistent consequences for lying and stealing, helping her restate what she wants in a way other than whining—all help to stop these typical Adventurous-age issues.

You also have the delightful job of teaching her things that will foster her growth in life and in relationships. She learns manners from you, which ultimately serve to help her love and encourage others. She learns responsibilities, which help her learn to be considerate and not take advantage of those around her. This is also the time most parents choose to talk to their daughters about sex, which can be a rich time to teach your child about the miracle of new life.

In these six-to-eleven years, your daughter is much like a coming-of-age movie. She is out riding her bike through puddles and stirring up all kinds of adventures with her buddies, but as soon as you open that screen door and call her home, she knows where she belongs.

Your Adventurous-age daughter has other voices in her life, but for now, yours is the loudest, and you have the fearfully delightful job of using that voice to call out in her truths about herself, about life, and about God that help her become more of who he is creating her to be.

CHAPTER 4

The Narcissistic Years: Twelve to Fifteen

Cherylanne is fourteen, and she is pretty. I am twelve and I am not, although Cherylanne said this is the awkward stage and I could just as likely get better. We watch.

ELIZABETH BERG, *DURABLE GOODS*

It is easy to picture this moment ... maybe because it has happened in your own home. Two girls are sitting on a bed, holding up a mirror. The older girl, Cherylanne is trying to help the younger one, Katie, "look better" ... fixing her makeup and hair, showing her what clothes she should and shouldn't wear.

Cherylanne is helping Katie out of what she believes is the kindness of her heart. In her narcissistic world, it is kind to tell a friend that she is awkward but will get better.

Katie feels shamefully appreciative. She doesn't know how to dress "cool" or wear her makeup "right." She doesn't like the way she looks. But Cherylanne knows how to do these things. Cherylanne can help, even if Katie feels a little hurt by the way she sometimes says things.

Recently a mom told us that she loves to drive her daughter and friends home from school. She has figured out how to turn the car stereo so it is louder in the back, causing the girls to have to speak up to hear each other over the music. This gives her the best eavesdropping capabilities. She said that conversations frequently begin with "I don't want to be mean but ..." The statements that follow are similar to Cherylanne's—told out of the goodness of the speaker's narcissistic heart—focused on what other people think but unaware of how other people feel.

We recently asked a group of twelve- to fifteen-year-old girls what they were most worried about. These are their answers.

- Girls talking about me
- What other people think about whatever you're doing
- If my friends are really going to be my friends around other people
- If I get in a fight with my friends, are we going to hate each other and become rivals?
- Spiders
- Grades
- Boys
- Friend situation (who is being mean)
- Rumors
- Succeeding in school and in general
- Trying to be good at everything
- Trying to make myself worth someone's time
- Fighting with siblings
- Loneliness
- Screwing up my life and not realizing it
- That people will think I'm weird
- Not making the right choices
- Gaining weight
- If people judge me from my appearance
- That I won't know how to get out of a bad situation
- Getting in trouble

Almost every answer these girls gave has to do with two things: first, what other people think about me, and second, what I think about me. Notice that both sentences end in *me*.

Girls in the Narcissistic Years are preoccupied with themselves. Mark Twain said that children should be nailed into a pickle barrel at age twelve, fed through a knothole, and not let out until age twenty. He must have parented a girl in her Narcissistic Years or at least known the most obvious side of girls from twelve to fifteen.

As she approaches middle school, your daughter undergoes a significant transformation. Her looks don't change as drastically as in the previous two stages, but her behavior does. She comes home from school and goes directly to her room. Her two favorite possessions move quickly from the doll and gun of the Adventurous Years to a cell phone and the Internet. Friends become all-important—oh, and her hair. She spends an inordinate amount of time in the bathroom.

Remember in chapter 2 when we named the culprit for a majority of the problems that arise in the life of a girl? *Development.* These changes have everything to do with development for your daughter. Believe it or not, there are spiritual, emotional, and even physical reasons for these changes. God is still growing your daughter—even though, at times, it seems like someone much more diabolical has taken over. But these changes are necessary. She is becoming her own person. She is developing her own opinions and tastes, or at least transferring them away from you. In the process of finding her own voice, your daughter will often take up the voices of her peers first. But she will find her own and is moving in that direction during these Narcissistic Years.

That is the obvious side of girls from twelve to fifteen. But there are also changes that are not so obvious. The obvious changes feel hard, even painful as a parent. The Narcissistic Years are ones in which you feel rejected a great deal. We talk more about this later in the book as we look more closely at the relationships between girls and parents.

But there are also changes going on, a little past the surface, that are much more hopeful. A girl's brain changes significantly as new growth takes place and those dreaded hormones work their magic. Her emotions become like shifting sands as the hormones exert their control over your adolescent daughter. Thankfully, however, she is stirring spiritually in ways that are momentous. God is giving her the ability to seek and know him at deeper levels, and, sometimes, that is enough hope to hang on to through the more obvious, painful changes of these years.

PHYSICAL DEVELOPMENT

The psychologist Michael Gurian calls this age the "most frightening episode of life a girl will experience," and with good reason. As a parent, you see her narcissism, you see her moodiness and her irritability, and you hear in her voice her insecurities about friends ... or boys ... or both. From twelve to fifteen years of age, your daughter has an excuse. Well, maybe not an excuse, because there are ways to challenge the behaviors and attitudes that often permeate adolescence, but there is a biological reason for the tumultuousness of her behavior and emotions during these Narcissistic Years.

Hiccups in Confidence

Your daughter's brain is undergoing a revolution. Whereas growth slows down during her Adventurous Years, the connections in her brain grow as fast in these twelve-to-fifteen years as they did in infancy.

From a scientific standpoint, what is happening is this: The *prefrontal cortex* is like the president of your daughter's brain corporation. It is the portion of her brain that manages her moods, regulates her memory, and helps her with skills such as organization and planning. Until recently, it was believed that babies' brains were developed by the time they were five or six. Structurally, this is true. But the connections (*synapses*) between the cells begin a period of rapid growth again around puberty.

From a practical standpoint, what is happening is this: A girl's brain is on overload from age twelve to fifteen. In essence, it overwhelms itself. This leads to several results, the first of which we will call "hiccups in confidence."

On any given day, as you pick your daughter up from school, she might be sad ... with no apparent cause. She may wake up one morning (or many mornings) feeling bad about herself. These are hiccups in confidence.

Because the brain is changing so rapidly, it is as if it malfunctions. The result is that your daughter feels bad about herself when nothing has happened.

On the other hand, there are a number of adolescent girls who struggle with depression. We see many of them in our offices. In fact, depression is often hard to diagnose in adolescent girls because adolescence itself mimics so many of the symptoms of clinical depression.

I (Sissy) recently told a group of juniors and seniors in high school about hiccups in confidence. As I explained this phenomenon, there was a collective "OHH" in the room. "Is that why seventh grade was so horrible for every girl we know?"

Most of the time, girls will point to seventh grade as the hardest grade they ever lived through. Hiccups in confidence is just one of the reasons.

Nearsightedness

Not only are the brain connections growing rapidly in a girl age twelve to fifteen, but hormones are beginning to take center stage. This adds to a girl's sense of being overwhelmed and markedly limits her perceptive abilities.

As we said before, she is thinking about herself continually—who she is, how she looks, and what other people think about who she is and how she looks—but there is a significant problem: she is terribly "nearsighted."

I (Melissa) remember riding on a bus to a retreat in ninth grade. I was trying to go to sleep and hadn't quite gotten there yet. My friends behind me started talking.

"Is Melissa ever serious or does she just joke around all the time?"

I remember being so surprised and not realizing they saw me like that.

The changes in the brains of adolescent girls cause this kind of nearsightedness. Studies show that, between the ages of twelve and fourteen, a teenager's ability to pick up on social cues and to distinguish emotions such as anger and sadness drops significantly. What this means is that your daughter is not trying to ignore your subtle hints that you are disappointed. She often does not notice when your voice drops or when your facial expression changes. Her brain is so preoccupied that she simply misses it.

In their all-important social world, this causes trouble for girls. They desperately want to be liked by their peers. One girl may try to be funny to impress her friends, but with her nearsightedness, she doesn't know when to stop, and the other girls quickly grow tired. Another girl may try to do things for her friends, such as decorate their lockers or help them with homework, but rather than making herself indispensable, she ingratiates herself, and other girls are annoyed.

While there may be nothing we can do to prevent hiccups in confidence, we can help the nearsightedness of Narcissistic-age girls. In our groups at Daystar, response is one of the most important elements. Seventh- and eighth-grade groups do not respond to each other naturally. One of the girls will walk into group and say, "My dad left us last night." How do the other girls respond? They don't ... they stare.

This doesn't last long, however. "How do you all think Jill is feeling? What would you feel if you were Jill? What do you want to say to her?" one of us will quickly ask. Basically, we have to teach them to respond.

What happens next, however, is funny. One thirteen-year-old will turn to Jill and say, "I'm so sorry your dad left. You must be really mad at him." Then she will immediately turn to whichever one of us is leading the group and smile. Unlike girls in our older high school groups, if they do respond, these Narcissistic-age girls respond because they are supposed to. They respond to please, not out of genuine caring for one of their friends.

This will change. Compassion will reemerge in your daughter. She will be able to pick up on social cues and recognize emotions in others. But for now, it is enough to help nearsighted girls know that there is something far off—even if she can't see it herself.

Well-Worn Paths

In the last chapter, we talked about the importance of activities for girls. These activities aid in a phenomenon psychologist Gerald May talks about in his insightful book *Addiction and Grace*: "the well-worn path."

As a new activity is learned, a neural pathway is created. The more often that activity is participated in, the more well-worn that particular neural pathway becomes. It's a lot like the road home—how sometimes you'll end up in your driveway when you really meant to drive to the store. It's a well-worn path.

These well-worn paths in the brain are often established before or during the Narcissistic Years. This is why children who learned to play the piano—or ride a bike—or a host of other activities—before the age of sixteen can pick it back up much easier as an adult than someone who tried to learn these activities later in life.

The path concept is both a strength and a weakness for Narcissistic-age girls. If you want your daughter to be able to participate in certain activities, and even find some confident enjoyment in them, give her opportunities to participate in these activities during her Narcissistic Years. She may likely choose to quit piano or dance lessons as a twelve- to fifteen-year-old, but she will have formed a path that she can come back to without much difficulty.

These paths can also become destructive. Addictions, according to May, are essentially well-worn paths. Statistically, most addictions find their beginnings in adolescence. Your daughter is trying to find her own identity. She is motivated by a desire to "live on the edge." And her brain is predisposed to these well-worn paths—whether they are healthy or destructive. We talk more about these addictive behaviors in chapter 9.

The Insurgence of Hormones—a.k.a. Puberty

"Surely, she hasn't entered puberty yet."

We hear these words often from parents of Narcissistic-age girls. They are said with a little hope, a little hesitancy, and a lot of trepidation. Puberty can be a dreaded word for parents—and understandably so. Puberty wreaks havoc on the brain of your daughter and often the peace of your home.

In the Adventurous Years hormones began to enter the brains of girls. It is in these Narcissistic Years that they take center stage. As the hormones surge through your daughter's brain, puberty begins. In his book, *The Wonder of Girls*, psychologist Michael Gurian has compiled this list of all that puberty affects in the life of your daughter:

- her moods
- the words she uses, her speed of conversation, her need for conversation
- how she'll do on tests at a given time of the month
- how much she'll eat
- how she'll relate to people nonverbally
- how she'll feel about the people she loves
- how she'll see herself fitting in
- her self-esteem
- her level of competitiveness
- her social ambition

- her aggression
- her primary emotions, like joy, anger, and grief

Basically, hormones affect just about everything in a girl's life besides the color of her eyes. Thankfully, our culture is giving more and more credibility to the effect of hormones on women. These effects are also true—and often especially true—in the life of your Narcissistic-age girl. Her period most likely begins and is becoming regulated during these years—and, until it does, hormones will take center stage in her and often your life.

The onset of puberty often accompanies the onset of an interest in her sexuality. Boys offer more than just adventure and friendship—they now offer allure and intrigue. Spin the bottle, five minutes in heaven, and other kissing games go on at parties. Stolen kisses take place under the bleachers, and notes are passed back and forth ... back and forth ... back and forth ... with questions and boxes to choose answers. (Actually, notes today take place more on the Internet than they do on notebook paper.) To top off all of that, boys at this age are experiencing five to seven surges of testosterone each day ... which adds to the confusion and overwhelmed feelings of these twelve-to-fifteen years, for everyone involved.

In chapter 9, we will look more deeply at sexuality, promiscuity, and Internet relationships in the lives of girls, and we will also look at what you as a parent can do to help your daughter navigate all of these complex challenges facing her in her Narcissistic Years.

With all the hormones raging, the brain connections growing, and the confidence hiccupping, it is a wonder that the brains of narcissistic girls don't explode. Actually, it is not their brains that explode but—as many parents of Narcissistic-age girls can attest—their emotions.

EMOTIONS AND PERSONALITY DEVELOPMENT

By the time a girl reaches her Narcissistic Years, her personality has mostly developed—but then it changes. In her Adventurous Years, your daughter wanted to go to the movies with you. Now she wants you to drop her off a block away. Before, she would actually tell you about her day when you picked her up from school. Now she speaks in one-word utterances.

Your relationship with her seems to have changed—overnight. Her peers have taken on a whole new level of importance—overnight. And she tries to emulate older high school girls ... other women she thinks are cool ... anyone, it seems, except you.

Just what is happening to the girl you love? We already know there is a lot going on in her brain. But there is also a great deal taking place in her emotions and personality development. And it all has to do with her relationships.

The three relational areas of most importance to girls in the Narcissistic Years are

- her parents
- her peers
- other voices

In chapter 7, we will come back to the idea and the necessity of other voices in the lives of girls. But, for now, we'll let her tell us what is happening in her own words in the world of her parents and her peers.

- "Whatever ..."
- "What up, dude?"

"Whatever ..."—The World of Parents

The first morning of every camp, we have the kids answer several questions to give them a chance to get to know each other. One of the questions is "Who in your life has impacted you the most?" During fifth-and-sixth-grade camp, almost every girl will say her mom. During seventh-and-eighth-grade camp, almost none will.

Welcome to the world of parents for Narcissistic-age girls. What is happening in this world? Her answer would be "whatever ..."

"Honey, do you want to go to the store with your dad?"

"Whatever."

◎

"Do you want broccoli with your chicken?"

"Whatever."

◎

"You're grounded for talking that way to your mother."

"Whatever."

Thankfully, many kids are not allowed to use this word with their parents, because of the degree of disrespect it carries. But even those who don't say it aloud are often saying it in their minds.

Why "whatever"? What does it mean? "Whatever" subtly implies three components that characterize a girl's relationship to her parents in these years:

- independence
- ambivalence
- awareness

Independence

From age twelve to fifteen, girls are trying to establish their independence. They are trying to discover who they are as separate from you—their parent.

An adult trying to become more independent would find outside interests. They would spend time with other people—do things as an individual, as well as a couple. A wife might take a girls' trip to the beach. A husband might go on a fishing trip, or vice versa.

Adolescents don't have these kinds of choices. They can't just decide to take a trip with friends or take up painting—unless mom will drive them to art class.

So their choices come in other ways. Narcissistic-age girls assert their independence in what room they choose to spend the evening (usually theirs). They control how much they're willing to communicate with parents (usually not very).

Girls in these years need the freedom to be independent—within boundaries. Many girls tell us they're so overwhelmed with trying to have friends at school that they need a little time to themselves when they come home. When a girl's mom follows her into her room asking, "What's wrong?" it takes away a small portion of her independence.

Your daughter needs time to herself. She is formulating her own opinions, ideas, and preferences—and needs to do so in these years. This is not a rejection of you or all that you've taught her growing up. This is her becoming her own person. Let her go to her room. And then, after a little while, invite her to go on a walk or go to the neighborhood coffee shop—or make sure she comes to family dinner. Draw her back out in relationship. She actually wants both—even though it may not look like it.

Ambivalence

A fourteen-year-old girl I (Melissa) counsel can't seem to talk about anything other than her mother. Every week she recounts their latest argument, including all of her mother's recent transgressions. As she talks, it is as if anger, frustration, and disdain for her mother oozes out of her very being.

Recently, as I waited with her to be picked up from group, her cell phone rang. She answered it and said, "Hi, Mommy. Okay ... I'm downstairs. See you in a minute. I love you."

I was shocked. But then I remembered the ambivalence of twelve- to fifteen-year-old girls. They are like toddlers wandering away and looking back at their parents.

A father of a fifteen-year-old recently told us that his daughter asked him to tuck her in. "You know, Dad, you don't have many years left of this," she told him. Of course, this dad trotted straight upstairs—but we can almost guarantee that the first words out of her mouth the next morning were the beginnings of an argument.

Come close ... get away. Teenage girls are saying both. I need independence because I'm trying to find myself, but I also need you. It is important to remember they want both. Their "get aways" are more about them than they are about you—even when their words seem directed at you.

Awareness

In these twelve-to-fifteen years, the thinking of girls becomes more abstract (which we talk more about in the section on spiritual development). They are able to see into situations and into people with a little more awareness, but this awareness is clouded by their narcissism.

So the sixth grader who wanted to be just like you six months ago starts to point out your imperfections. Her thinking is abstract enough to notice them but idealistic enough to think they shouldn't be there.

Twelve-year-old Katie is in the middle of this kind of awareness—and so is her mother, by default. Her mother is engaging, kind, helpful, and highly productive, and her daughter is hot on her trail. "My mom is so frustrating. I feel like all she does is criticize me. She tells me what I'm doing wrong—when I see her doing the same things. My grandmother told me I am at an age where I'm going to start to notice things more. I wish my mom would just stop."

This well-meaning grandmother was right. Girls in this age

do notice more—and they can either use this awareness for good or for evil. Katie was using it for evil—or at least to criticize her mom.

But again, they're ambivalent. I (Sissy) talked to this girl about her relationship with her mom. What I wanted to say was, "Quit being so critical of your mom. Do you have any idea all that she does for you?" But as we know, that would have gone nowhere. So, instead, I tried to help her see the unrealistic expectations she was placing on her mother. I had her revisit the situation and think through it from a little different perspective. "Tell me about a time you felt like your mother was being critical. What did you say? What did she say? What do you think you were communicating to her? What do you think she was realy feeling toward you when that happened? What could your mom have done differently in that situation? What would you have done?"

As this girl rehearsed the scene for me, she realized that she was the one who was frustrated with herself. It wasn't that her mom was being overly critical—she was actually being overly critical of her mom. As this awareness dawned on her, she was filled with genuine regret.

We believe this is the real heart of twelve- to fifteen-year-old girls: they are aware but narcissistic. They argue and push away but want to be tucked in.

All this is necessary in the life of your girl. She needs to become independent, ambivalent, and aware. As she does so, things will most likely get tougher at home. She will argue with you, be disappointed, cause conflict. But working through (notice we didn't say ignoring) these conflicts gives her a tool that will be invaluable to her as she grows older. She will learn to handle her anger and deal with disappointments, and she will learn to forgive and offer grace.

Parenting a twelve-to-fifteen-year-old is often a painful process. She is moving away from you and toward her friends. She will come back. But first, she has to make a sojourn into the land of giggles, clothes, makeup, and other girls.

"What Up, Dude?"—The World of Friendships

> *"Friendships are so much harder for girls. We have to try to make other girls like us. We have to be really nice. Boys just play basketball, say, 'What up, dude?' and they're friends."*
>
> AN ELEVEN-YEAR-OLD

This statement was one girl's feeling on the hardest part of being a girl. Girls expend an enormous amount of energy from twelve to fifteen making and maintaining friendships.

Friendships take on a whole new level of importance in the life of a Narcissistic-age girl. Several years ago, a family came in for counseling with three girls. One was in fifth grade, one in seventh, and one in tenth. The parents were getting a divorce. The youngest and the oldest daughters were torn up about it. For their first appointment, all they could do was cry. The middle daughter in seventh grade, however, was entirely different. She came in and told us she was fine with her parents' divorce. What she really wanted to talk about was her friend who was mad at her.

The middle daughter did grieve her parents' divorce—several years later, once she had moved out of her Narcissistic Years, but in those years her friendship difficulties superseded those of her family.

We talk a lot with parents of Narcissistic-age girls about how their voices become quieter while peers' voices become louder, and it is in these years that this principle takes effect. When she's not with her friends, she's talking to them on the phone or on the Internet, or she's text messaging them. When she's not talking to them, she's trying to talk you into letting her talk to them.

Friends also have a great deal of power in these years. They can make a girl feel "chosen" one minute and dashed on the rocks the next, and this is often how it works: best friends on Monday, not speaking on Tuesday.

An eighteen-year-old recently told us, "When I was twelve, my mom used to get mad at any friend who hurt my feelings. The next day at school we'd make up and be best friends again. And then my mom wouldn't let her spend the night that weekend. I had to tell her over and over that's just the way girls are. They're fickle."

They are terribly fickle in these years. Most girls will be on the giving and the receiving end at some point between the ages of twelve and fifteen. The givers feel too much power, while the receivers feel too little. All of them, however, are acting out of a place of insecurity.

Every girl we have met in her Narcissistic Years feels like an outsider at some point. She feels like everyone else shares a secret or a joke that she isn't privy to. Every girl takes things personally from other peers. And most girls would rather impress their peers than be individuals.

I (Melissa) remember going for a walk with my two "coolest" friends in the eighth grade. To get to where we were going, we had to cross a creek. Being the confident, long-legged girls they were, this was not a problem, but my legs—and my confidence—were not quite so ample. I tried to get them to go ahead, knowing that I could scramble my way across as long as they weren't watching, but they patiently waited for me. I jumped, barely making it across, and broke my arm. They had no idea. Nauseated and reeling from the pain, I carried that arm around all afternoon like nothing was wrong. Nothing could have been more important for me than impressing my friends.

Often, in these years, your daughter will have similar priorities. In chapter 7, we will look more deeply into the relational world of girls. We will talk about what helps and what doesn't as your daughter navigates the murky waters of peer relationships.

And finally, we'll tell you how to utilize this all-important world to help her become more of who God is calling her to be.

Girls are relational beings. Their hunger for relationships increases exponentially during these years. It will be obvious as you watch their friendships. But even though it is not quite so obvious, they are also hungry for a relationship with you. Most importantly, they are becoming hungry for a relationship with God in ways that are richer and deeper than ever before.

SPIRITUAL DEVELOPMENT

> *"What do I do? Where do I go? I'm so lost. I really do focus on God, but I seem to be walking in circles. Aren't you supposed to move straight ahead with God? Am I doing something wrong? Probably. I always do."*

These are the words of a girl in her Narcissistic Years. She wants a relationship with God but doesn't feel like she can get it right. She sees her own failure and is angry with herself for being such a mess.

In the midst of her frustration, the desire of this young girl is to live a redeemed, relational life—both with God and with people. In this section, we look more closely at these three key words in the spiritual lives of girls:

- messy
- redemptive
- relational

Messy

I (Melissa) usually meet with a child the first time they come to Daystar. During this appointment they tell me why they think their parents brought them to counseling, and I tell them a little bit about us. At the end of the conversation, I usually say, "Let's go ahead and get this out in the open: You're a mess." I quickly add, "So am I. Everyone here is. You'll be a *loved* mess at Daystar." As I say these words, sixteen- and seventeen-year-olds smile. Thirteen- and fourteen-year-olds look shocked. They can't believe anyone would say that out loud.

Several summers ago a girl came to camp who had every appearance of being perfect. She looked good, smiled all of the time, and was well-liked by everyone who met her. During camp we went to see the newest Star Wars movie. Afterward, we had a conversation about the "dark side" in each of us. As I (Melissa) was teaching, I turned to this girl and said something like, "Even Elizabeth has a dark side." Elizabeth looked at me with that same shocked expression that girls get in their first appointment.

The next night Elizabeth came up to me before our meeting. "Melissa, no one has ever told me I had a dark side before. You're right. I do ... I know I do. I just have been afraid to admit it."

At the end of camp, Elizabeth's mom came to pick her up. I made a joke in front of her about Elizabeth's dark side. I quickly found the origins of the shocked look. Her mom replied, "Elizabeth is sweet. I don't know what you're talking about. She doesn't have a dark side."

Her mom was afraid Elizabeth would feel bad about what I had said, but Elizabeth and I knew something different. She was (and still is) a mess, and we both knew it, and Elizabeth was a freer, more honest child after her *messiness* was out in the open.

The reason girls in this age often look shocked is that they can't believe anyone knows their secret. In her Adventurous Years your daughter's thinking was concrete. She most likely tried her best to be good or funny or act in whatever her chosen strategy was for staying out of the coatroom. Her thinking was black-and-white enough to believe that her strategy, for the most part, worked.

But as she reaches the Narcissistic Years, things change significantly. Her thinking becomes abstract. It is as if her eyes are being opened to the realities of life around and inside of her. Nothing makes sense in quite the way it used to. Rote answers don't take away her questions, or her insecurities. People disappoint her, and she disappoints herself.

What does this abstract thinking do for the faith of your daughter? It creates a hotbed for spiritual growth. What better way to understand our need for Christ than to know our messiness? In these twelve-to-fifteen years, girls are better able to understand their sin (or messiness) than ever before, and with that new understanding comes a much deeper awareness of their need for redemption.

Redemptive

Several years ago, a fifteen-year-old girl came to camp who had never been to Daystar. Laura was brought to counseling because of her explosive anger at home. Her teachers said she was a model student. She was well-liked by her peers at school. All of her disappointment, hurt, and anger was stored up during the day and poured out at home each night. Her parents were not only concerned—they were exhausted.

Through the beginning of the ten-day term, Laura was delightful. She quickly developed friendships with the other girls. She was helpful, kind, and encouraging. But on the seventh day, something shifted. Laura's responses grew shorter and had an edge. That afternoon, we had our traditional sixteen-mile bike ride. When Laura couldn't get her gears to work properly, she snapped. She yelled at several of the girls around her, threw down her bike, and stormed off.

That night, we gathered as a group for worship. Up until this week, Laura had never really bought into her parents' faith. As we began reminiscing about our day, Laura spoke up. "I didn't really want to come to camp. My parents told me Daystar was Christian and counseling, and I didn't want either one. But something happened to me today. I was a brat out there on the bike ride.

And you all were kind. Even though I yelled, you stayed with me and wanted to help. You didn't go away because I was rude, even though I probably deserved it. It's one thing to be loved when you are nice, but it's a whole other thing to still be loved when you're a brat."

That day was a turning point for Laura. She accepted Christ the next evening. And she went back to that day as her first real understanding of redemption. Laura felt loved in spite of her messiness—her sin. God's redemption seeped through the other girls who stayed with her in her anger. Their love for her paved the way for God's redemptive love to work in Laura's heart.

One of the kids' favorite hymns at camp is "Amazing Love" by Charles Wesley. Listen to the words and you will understand why.

He left his father's throne above;
So free, so infinite his grace,
Emptied himself of all but love
And bled for Adam's helpless race
'Tis mercy all, immense and free;
For O, my God, it found out me!
Amazing love, how can it be that
Thou, my God, should die for me?

This song, and in particular this verse, speaks to the redeeming love that girls from twelve to fifteen desire so desperately: "'Tis mercy all, immense and free, for O, my God, it found out me!"

Being found out is much like Melissa pointing out Elizabeth's dark side or Laura being loved in spite of her anger. These girls long for a redemptive love.

It is not a coincidence that we have more children say that they want to experience a relationship with Christ in seventh- and eighth-grade camp than any other. These adolescents are aware of their sin—their messiness—and they are longing to be loved in spite of that messiness, in ways that are both redemptive and relational.

Relational

One of the most common phrases for girls to say to each other in these twelve-to-fifteen years is, "What's wrong?" In their Adventurous Years, girls didn't say these kinds of things. If her friend was sad, your daughter drew her a picture or tried to make her laugh. As they reach the Narcissistic Years, however, girls ask. When one of their friends is sad, they ask what is wrong (often ad nauseum) and usually believe the answer has something to do with them. This has to do with the relational nature of girls in their Narcissistic Years.

Girls are desperate for relationships at this age, and they want to experience these relationships. They want to feel close to their friends—if they don't, there must be a problem. The same holds true for their relationship with God.

Several years ago I (Sissy) was meeting with a girl in eighth grade who had doubts about her faith. I asked Amanda to take some time before our next meeting to write down all the reasons she doubted.

> What if God isn't real, then what would happen if I died?
>
> If he is real then why do I always get down and go through hard things?
>
> Sometimes I say, "God, if you're there give me a sign" and I never seem to get one.
>
> Why, whenever I call out to God, he never answers?
>
> I know that no one is worthy, but why do I feel that I am the most unworthy?

These were Amanda's reasons for her doubt. We also believe that one of the main reasons Amanda doubted was that her black-and-white, concrete-thinking faith of her Adventurous Years was no longer working. She needed a faith that moved beyond the black-and-white to incorporate all the abstract, relational thoughts that were swimming around inside her head.

As you read her list, you can see the relational need in it. Friendships are important to Amanda, but she also deeply wants relationship with God. She wants him to show up for her in a way that is relational. What Amanda really wants from God is much the same as what she wants from her friends: she wants to experience him.

Like Thomas, girls in their Narcissistic Years want to touch the holes in Jesus' hands and side, which is why girls come home so often talking about a retreat in which "everyone cried." It is why things like nailing sins to a cross or washing feet have such meaning for twelve-to-fifteen-year-old girls. Girls want to know Jesus in a way that is more of a reality than an idea.

Last summer I (Melissa) taught on Judges 7:16–20. In these verses, God gave Gideon instructions on defeating the Midianites. Every one of Gideon's men was supposed to take into battle a horn, a torch, and a pot. The torch was to be kept in a pot until the given time. At that time, Gideon's men were instructed to smash their pots, shine their lights, blow their horns, and shout.

So we talked about pots and torches. An earthen pot symbolizes who we are and what we do to cover that up. Some of the girls talked about doing whatever they could to fit in. Others talked about trying to be perfect or look like they had it all together. Still others talked about trying to be cool—sarcastic and unaffected by things that hurt them.

The next night, when we got together, we had a stack of clay pots sitting up front. After worship, we gave the kids an opportunity to come and take a pot. One by one, each child at camp came to the front of the room and talked about what his or her pot was. She then took that pot, went out to the driveway, and smashed it.

The next night, each child came again to the front of the room. On this night, we talked about lights. Now that the pots were broken, the lights of these kids could shine. So, one by one, the group talked about what the light of each camper looked like.

"Betsie's light is her kindness. She doesn't have to say much, but every time I see her, she is encouraging someone."

@

"Clare's light is her sense of humor. No matter how sad I am, she always makes me laugh."

And on and on until every camper was talked about. Gideon's story spoke to all three of the spiritual needs of girls in their Narcissistic Years. It acknowledged their messiness by giving them a chance to talk about what each of their pots were. It was redemptive in that it is the light that shines out through the broken pots. And it was deeply relational. It was relational with the kids in that they were given an opportunity to encourage each other.

Almost a year later, I (Melissa) received a note. It said,

Melissa,

Several of the girls really want to smash pots again this summer at camp.

Please consider it.

Sincerely, Anne and Ellie

Anne and Ellie wanted to re-smash pots because this teaching touched on these three vital needs in the spiritual lives of girls. Girls need to be able to connect with God in ways that acknowledge their messiness, that are redemptive, and that are relational. When, as adults, we teach them with words and experience, we give them opportunities to know God's love in a way they couldn't until this stage of their development.

God is using who your daughter is and what she needs in these years—even when all you sometimes see, as a parent, is her messiness. And that hope is something to hang on to.

But what can you do past hanging on? How can you connect with her when she feels unconnectable? The answer lies in an approach we call the "back door."

PARENTING DURING THE NARCISSISTIC YEARS: THROUGH THE BACK DOOR

Several years ago, we wrote a book called *The Back Door to Your Teen's Heart*. The "back door" is our parenting philosophy for Narcissistic-age kids. Why the back door? Because the front door simply doesn't work with teenagers.

To the degree that kids can predict you, they will dismiss you. Any parent of a girl between twelve and fifteen has felt dismissed—by either a look, a grunt, or a "whatever." To come in the front door often earns an immediate dismissal.

A fifteen-year-old recently told us about a father-daughter conference she attended. Halfway through the conference, the speaker told the fathers to turn toward their daughters. They were to look their daughters in the eyes and say, "You are beautiful."

You can imagine this young girl's reaction. "It was so stupid. Not only did I feel dumb, but my dad didn't even mean it. They told him to say it."

This was a front-door approach. A back-door approach might be something more like, "Honey, your mom's birthday is coming up. You have such great style. I would love for you to help me choose some clothes for her."

The back door invites your teenager to relationship, rather than commanding it. It is unpredictable. If you pick your daughter up from school and ask her how her day was, you already know the answer you are going to get—"Fine"—and she knows you are going to ask the question.

Instead, ask her something different. Ask her what the cafeteria served for lunch, or ask her if she could go anywhere in the world right then, where would she go and why? And you can always ask about her friends—not in a way that makes her think you are trying to get information, but in a way that lets her know you genuinely care about them. "You said Sally just found out her mom has cancer. How was she today?" Be unpredictable. She is much more likely to participate in a conversation when you relate to her in a way she doesn't expect.

The back door takes a little more creativity but gives you a better chance to connect without being dismissed. A great back-door approach is to talk with your daughter while doing something else. We often have the best talks with kids at this age sitting on the dock at camp or on the pontoon boat. Make cookies with your daughter. Watch one of her favorite movies. Play basketball with her and engage her in conversation while you're shooting. A fourteen-year-old recently told us that her favorite things her parents do are "drive, shop, and love." The driving and shopping are also back-door type activities.

Girls in these twelve-to-fifteen years are narcissistic. They are awkward and unsure of themselves—which really makes them unsure of everything else. This is often especially true of their relationship with us. It's not cool as a fourteen-year-old to be close to your mom, but, as we sneak around and come in the back door, they are caught off guard. They are often talking to us without even realizing it. They are relating and allowing us to drive, shop, and love them through these Narcissistic Years.

CHAPTER 5

The Autonomous Years: Sixteen to Nineteen

In all of women's descriptions (of themselves), identity is defined in a context of relationship and judged by a standard of responsibility and care.

CAROL GILLIGAN, *IN A DIFFERENT VOICE*

One of my (Sissy's) strongest memories of my junior year in high school was with my friend Tracey. We were both privileged to be a part of a group of nine girls who were fun, kind, and very serious about our faith. We would pray together often and were committed to doing the "right things"—that is, not doing the "wrong things"—like drinking, smoking, and so on. We were what you would consider "good girls." And, much like the quote above by Carol Gilligan, our identities had much to do with relationship and what we believed to be—and not to be—our responsibilities.

I remember one afternoon when Tracey and I decided to go together to a Christian bookstore. We spent a long time browsing through the books and music and finally bought a Twila Paris CD. I remember sitting in Tracey's car that afternoon being very moved by a song called *The Warrior is a Child*. Then Tracey and I prayed together. It was an intense spiritual and relational experience with a dear friend.

The catch was that this took place at about 1:30 on a Thursday afternoon, which is significant primarily because, as Tracey and I sobbed over Twila in the car, our names were being called in the roll for chemistry class.

We had skipped class to go to the Christian bookstore and pray together. What kind of irony is that? It is just the kind of irony that girls in their Autonomous Years live in the midst of.

We took ourselves very seriously. We believed we had the freedom to do as we chose. The rules didn't necessarily apply to us—because we were doing something "right." We were finding our own voices—who we were, what we believed in. Not to mention the fact that what we were doing carried with it a little of an edgy thrill because it really was skipping class. We never even realized the hypocrisy of our situation.

From sixteen to nineteen, girls are becoming more autonomous. As our friend Pace said, "Wheels make all the difference." Those wheels take your daughter farther away from home and toward a far-off land—a land where she is able to make her own choices and become her own person, and that person, even in these years, is continuing to develop physically, emotionally, and spiritually.

PHYSICAL DEVELOPMENT

I (Sissy) recently had to send one of the girls I counsel to a residential treatment center for eating disorders. When I first met this intelligent, kind, engaging young woman, I tried as hard as I could to find some type of traumatic incident that was at the root of her problem. I asked her question after question about family issues, her past—any event that could have triggered her obsession with her body.

What I came to, however, was a shift in how she believed people saw her.

"When I was twelve and thirteen, people would talk all the time about how thin I was. They said I looked like an athlete.

They told me I was beautiful. And then, when I was around fifteen or sixteen, they stopped. No one said anything to me about the way I looked. So I knew I didn't look good anymore."

From twelve to sixteen, this young girl had gone through puberty. Normal changes had taken place in her body and in her brain.

Girls' brains and bodies are continuing to mature from sixteen to nineteen. This is an important season in a girl's development. It is one that shapes much of how they see themselves—not only now, but well into their adult lives.

Curves and Shame

We recently asked several of our friends how they felt about themselves, particularly their bodies, in the Autonomous Years. One answered before we had even finished the question: "I hated mine."

In these three words, she echoed what most girls in their Autonomous Years would say—if they felt the freedom to be honest. From sixteen to nineteen, the bodies of girls change—not in overwhelming ways, but in ways that are round and soft. Their prepubescent bodies are left behind for more curves—and often more shame, like the young woman with the eating disorder.

Think back on your own high school experience. How did you feel about your body? What about how you felt in comparison to your peers?

We talked in chapter 1 about being stuck at one developmental stage or other. We all can probably relate to being stuck here. Whether high school was a positive experience or a negative one, we were shaped by it. Actually, our shape during it has never left us. We still feel like the pudgy and awkward—or the lanky and clumsy—girl or whatever variation we felt we looked like in high school.

Whatever your daughter's body is like, she most likely feels awkward about it in her Autonomous Years, also. Prepubescent bodies are definitely the fashion, even though they are not reality. It is not your job, however, to make her lose weight (if she is overweight), unless she specifically asks. To make her weight loss your "project" without her request will only make her feel worse about herself.

What you can do is help her see the truth about who she is beyond what she looks like. You have a unique voice in her life to help her see how God has uniquely gifted her. We talk more about how you can do this in our final chapter.

She needs you. She needs your insight into who she is and who she can be. She needs your help in seeing that she has much more to offer than just her body—because, in these years, there will be those saying the opposite.

Sex and Confusion

"Sweet sixteen and never been kissed." These words used to be a phrase of endearment for teenage girls. Today, we don't really even hear the phrase. Part of the reason is that many girls have already been kissed by their sixteenth birthday. The other reason is that, for some girls who haven't, it is more of an embarrassment than an endearment. Sex is everywhere. Girls are overexposed, overstimulated, and tragically underestimated in this area.

The media portrays sex as the ultimate fulfillment of life for a teenager. Unfortunately, girls and boys are both exposed to this kind of media. Boys are led to believe that all girls would choose to be sexually active as teenagers if given the choice. These boys can be very persuasive, and are particularly so in the arena of sex. And girls can be very confused.

Without a doubt, girls' hormones add to this confusion. But while boys see sex as the end, girls see sex as the means. Like most elements of a girl's world, sex is relational. It is about intimacy. And there are biological reasons for this difference.

The primary hormones that exert control over a girl's brain

are estrogen, progesterone, and prolactin. Michael Gurian gives a detailed, insightful account of the science behind brain development in his book, *The Wonder of Girls*. This is our summary:

- **Estrogen** is the *nesting* hormone. It helps a girl/woman feel content with herself, her relationships, and her life.
- **Progesterone** is the *reassurance* hormone. It creates more of a need for connection and a need for that connection to be reinforced—often.
- **Prolactin** is the *inviting* hormone. Girls have 60 percent more of this hormone than boys. Basically, this hormone creates tear glands. It causes girls to cry, engendering empathy and inviting deeper connection.

Boys' brains, on the other hand, are exerting much higher levels of testosterone. Testosterone leads to independence and aggression and has much to do with the sexual drive of boys. Girls have some degree of testosterone, and boys have some degree of the predominant female hormones. But biologically, girls are wired to crave intimacy.

This combination can create large-scale, destructive confusion for all parties involved. A young woman I (Melissa) counsel recently told me she had sex for the first time. Angie was seventeen and was devastated. She had been told her entire life that sex was a sacred act that took place only in the context of marriage, but it had never made sense to her—until now.

"I wish someone had really told me why not to have sex. I know that God says not to, but I didn't really know why. It wasn't just to keep me from something fun—which is really what I thought. It was to protect me. It hurts so much now that Chad is gone. I knew he wasn't someone I needed to be with. But it is still so painful. I can't get over him. And now I know why."

Sex was relational for Angie, and it engaged her heart in a way that God reserved for marriage—for her protection. So how do we help girls like Angie? How do we give boundaries without them being a simplified list of dos and don'ts?

First, we can expose girls to something different. As a parent, you can teach your daughter the emotional realities of sex, but she needs to hear it from other voices, as well. She needs adults in her life, besides you, whom she respects and will speak these kinds of truths. She also needs friends who will encourage her and hold her accountable.

Girls need as many strong, honest voices as they can have. They need us to acknowledge the pressures and the allure of sex. They need to be able to speak to us openly about these things—knowing we will not "freak out." And they need us to speak truth to them—*after* we have heard and understood their perspective. They need our trust, our understanding, and our boundaries.

We talked to a young woman recently who said how helpful her youth group was in this area. She had a young woman who was discipling her who spoke with her group directly about sex. She said she always wanted to know "How far is too far?" (a question we hear a lot, by the way). The youth leaders were not afraid to answer that question.

"They told us anything beyond kissing was too far. My parents actually had a rule that I wasn't allowed to lay down on the couch with a boy. But I needed someone else telling me that too. I didn't always keep to that rule, but it helped to have one. I wanted to know when I was supposed to stop, and I wanted to know at what point I needed to ask forgiveness."

This honest young woman was glad for the boundaries in place both from her parents and her youth leaders. Because of the brain development of these autonomous girls, they are finally able to move out of narcissism enough to accept our guidance and attempt to handle these confusing situations.

Beyond Narcissism

A girl's brain slows back down in her Autonomous Years. The hiccups in confidence grow wider and wider apart. The nearsightedness begins to clear. Compassion reemerges. They are able to see another's perspective.

I (Sissy) met with a group of juniors and seniors in high school. I asked each of the girls to tell me what their parents' homes were like while they were growing up. Girl after girl told stories of hardship and loss. After the last one had finished, one of the girls made a statement that spoke volumes about the Autonomous Years: "It is amazing how many of our parents really had hard lives."

These girls had probably heard the same stories since they were young and had never thought a thing about them. But suddenly their parents were becoming more than just parents. They were becoming people. These seventeen- and eighteen-year-olds were able to take the perspective of their parents and see life through their eyes.

In their Autonomous Years, the brains of girls are even more capable of abstract thought. They are therefore able to understand their parents' perspective, and they are able to see how they themselves impact others. They can read facial expressions, see the hurt in a friend's eyes, and hear the disappointment in their teacher's voice.

Girls hunger for deeper relationships in these sixteen-to-nineteen years. They are biologically wired to give to others in ways that are more compassionate, more self-aware, and more abstract than ever before, and they are also able to do this with more logic and less emotion than they ever could have in those Narcissistic Years.

Gifts of the Frontal Lobe

I (Melissa) recently met with a seventeen-year-old alcoholic. This courageous young woman had been to ninety Alcoholics

Anonymous meetings in ninety days and was taking a long, hard look at her life. The word she had discovered that she believed best described her struggles was *impulsive*. She had been impulsive with alcohol, in relationships, and with her degree of responsibility toward life. She was ready for a change.

This is a girl in her Autonomous Years. For her to be self-aware enough to realize that she is impulsive typically takes the brain capabilities of a sixteen- to nineteen-year-old. But to want and implement change definitely requires the brain power—and brain structure of an Autonomous-age girl.

Scientists have recently discovered that the human brain does not finish its development until a person is in their mid-twenties. Your daughter's brain is much more developed at seventeen, however, than it was at fifteen. The frontal lobe is the last area of the brain to develop, controlling impulse, judgment, problem solving, and several other managerial-type activities.

So your daughter is better able to handle her emotions than ever before. She is not only able to see her destructive behavior, but also to change it. Even though she may not always act like it, she has the ability to reason. She can understand that actions have consequences and will avoid certain actions accordingly.

Most of these are new skills for your daughter—and God's timing—is providential. He is beginning to grow these abilities in your daughter while she is still under the safety of your roof and your widening boundaries.

Your daughter is becoming autonomous. She is physically and biologically predisposed to deeper relationships and toward living a more responsible life. She is becoming an adult—not just physically, but emotionally as well.

EMOTIONS AND PERSONALITY DEVELOPMENT

We have a friend named Bailey who is a goldendoodle. She is one of the newer, hybrid breeds of dog: half golden retriever, half standard poodle. She has the warmth and devotion of a golden, with all of the spunk, personality, and curls of a poodle. She is a great deal like your Autonomous-age daughter.

Your daughter is a hybrid as well. She is half girl, half woman in these sixteen-to-nineteen years. Her emotions are reflective of that mix. She wants independence but needs belonging. She wants to be admired by those close to her but is idealistic in terms of what that admiration looks like.

From sixteen to nineteen, your daughter's emotions and personality continue to mature, and as she matures, there are four statements that characterize her needs in the Autonomous Years.

- "Just trust me"
- "Pay attention to me"
- "I just want to be accepted"
- "That would never happen to me"

"Just Trust Me"—The Need for Independence

These sixteen-to-nineteen years are designed (at least, according to the government) to be the years girls (and boys) are given the keys to their independence. At sixteen they are given the literal keys to cars. At seventeen they can see R-rated movies. At eighteen they can buy cigarettes, join the military, drop out of school, and be emancipated from their parents.

To some degree, the founding fathers (and modern legislators as well as cigarette makers) believed that sixteen- through nineteen-year-olds are able to make their own decisions. As parents, this is hard to believe.

You know your daughter's lack of responsibility about her homework. You see that she still forgets to take out the trash and empty the dishwasher and even brush her teeth with any regularity. And you are fearful that she will be unprepared to handle life on her own—even when she puts up a mighty-big front.

But she wants to be independent. She wants to believe that you trust her—that you believe she is capable of things great and small. Mary Dea has just turned sixteen and has taken on a whole new level of familial responsibility. She drives her little sister to and from school and various activities. She helps her mom with errands. She is blossoming under the responsibilities that come with this kind of independence. It becomes her.

In reality, it is the trust of her parents just as much as her newfound independence that causes Mary Dea to blossom. We all remember girls who became destructive in the newfound freedom of their freshman year in college. Many of these girls didn't have the chance to succeed and fail in ever-widening boundaries. They were parented in the same manner throughout their entire high school experience and didn't gain any more responsibilities or earn any more privileges as they got older.

We offer a class for parents of juniors and seniors in high school with our friend and colleague David. One primary emphasis of this class is independence. Girls need more flexibility in determining their bedtimes for each year they progress through school. They need to be allowed a little more time on the phone and on the Internet. As they get older, their curfew needs to get a little later. As the freedoms increase in this way, the difference from high school to college is so negligible that the girls barely notice.

Girls need a chance to develop their independence. They need to be able to fail while they still live at home. During these years you can still meet them at the scene of their first fender bender. You can catch them as they come in with bloodshot eyes and alcohol on their breath. It is not your job to rescue them in these times, or they will not become independent. But you can be there to clean up the scrapes from the fall. You can sympathetically listen, ground them from the car if you need to, and ask them what they could do differently next time (back-door approach, remember?). And then you can remind them of all that you admire in them.

"Pay Attention to Me"—The Need for Admiration

> *How warm, though, things like admiration and appreciation made one feel, how capable of really deserving them, how different, how glowing. They seemed to quicken unsuspected faculties into life.... No wonder people liked admirers. They seemed, in some strange way, to make one come alive.*
>
> ELIZABETH VON ARNIM, *THE ENCHANTED APRIL*

We have a friend named Leanne who has gone on several girls' trips with us. On those trips we all read a lot—quite a lot. Leanne, after about an hour, gets bored. She then comes over to one of us, pokes us repeatedly with her finger, and says, "Pay attention to me."

Girls in their Autonomous Years may not be quite as bold as Leanne. More likely, they will sit on the kitchen countertop as you are preparing dinner. They will take out the trash before you ask. They may ask you to help them pick out a prom dress or maybe just scoot a little closer on the couch.

Whether they are subtle or obvious, these girls want your attention. They have a need for you to be interested in them; and they long for you to admire them and appreciate them.

These are deepening years for girls—years in which they develop more strength, more compassion, more tenderness. As we talk about in the spiritual development section, these girls are finding their own voice—who they are, what they believe, what they are passionate about. This voice, however, is new—and they are often tentative about expressing it.

That's where admiration comes in. Admiration—from you and others they care for—begins to take the blurriness of who they are becoming and brings it into focus. It makes them feel a little freer and walk a little taller.

Another friend has a father who understood this need during her growing up years. For as long as she lived at home, he had the same routine every time she walked down the staircase. It didn't matter if she was wearing sweats or a party dress. He would stop whatever he was doing, turn toward her, and whistle the theme song to Miss America.

Every time her father did this, he was saying to her, "I see you. You are delightful and worthy of my attention." She couldn't have verbalized this then, but she knew he was doing more than just whistling a tune that made her feel good. He was communicating to her that she was valuable enough to pay attention to. He was both appreciating and admiring her.

Your daughter in these years wants you to notice her, she wants you to listen and be interested in her, and she wants you to be proud and respect who she is becoming.

Point out her gentleness. Tell her you're proud when she has written something well or shown someone kindness—and tell her friends, too, when you see things in them.

It's tragic how many girls don't have an admirer. To be respected, appreciated, and noticed during these years serves to reinforce all God is doing in the lives of Autonomous-age girls.

"I Just Want to Be Accepted"—The Need to Belong

I don't feel like I belong here. I'm so alone ... even my best friend has moved away. Why do I not have any friends? Am I not a good enough person? Am I too fat? Am I too ugly? Am I just so annoying that no one wants to be around me? Will I ever feel that sense of belonging that I'm looking for?

From the journal of a sixteen-year-old

We spoke to two parents recently about their seventeen-year-old daughter, Kristy. She is floundering in relationships. She comes straight home from school while other girls are meeting for coffee. She stays in her room most Friday nights, and her phone hardly ever rings.

So Kristy's parents took her to a counselor, worried that she was depressed. What this counselor said to those concerned parents was something with which we profoundly disagree. "Kristy is okay. She is just different from other kids. We talked about it for a long time, and she said she doesn't need friends the way others do. I agree. I think she's doing just fine."

Kristy is bluffing. She is much more like the young woman who wrote her thoughts in the beginning of this section than someone who doesn't care about having friends. She fooled this counselor—and is most likely fooling herself. It would hurt too much for Kristy to admit she is missing something that all girls in their Autonomous Years desperately want—a place to belong.

Several years ago a sixteen-year-old named Martha came to Daystar in a similar state. Her mother believed she was depressed. She didn't have friends. She said her mom was her best friend (which is a great thing, by the way, as long as she's not there by default).

Martha met with a counselor several times and joined a group. She was involved in the group for several months before we broke for the summer. The next fall, Martha seemed entirely different. She looked more confident, didn't hide herself in the way she dressed, and smiled more. These are her words: "I never had a place where I felt like I could be myself. It helped me so much to meet with you guys every week and feel that you really liked me. Now I've joined the band, and I actually have friends. Group is what gave me the confidence to do it."

In group, Martha began to feel that she belonged. Much like admiration, that sense of belonging freed her to be more herself. It gave her a feeling of security and connection.

In her Narcissistic Years, your daughter wanted to be able to identify with a group that was popular—or athletic—or whatever she was hoping to be more like. But from sixteen to nineteen, she wants to belong. She wants to be a part of a group she can call "my best friends." She wants a "best friend" of her own, and she would probably love to have a boyfriend. It's not that she wants these things for the title—she wants them for the security and the connection.

Your daughter is tentatively becoming more of the woman God has created her to be in these years. To belong helps that woman emerge from her own insecurities and know she will be accepted.

"That Would Never Happen to Me"—The Need to Idealize

At sixteen, I (Melissa) had just gotten involved with my youth group. We had a great group, but we had one problem—we didn't have a youth director. So I decided to volunteer. I went to my minister one Sunday after church. "Listen, things are going great right now with the youth group, but we really need a youth director. I just wanted to let you know that, until you can find one, I would be happy to step in."

Obviously, I had no training. I hadn't even been a Christian for very long. But I saw a need and, with all the idealism that characterizes the Autonomous Years, I thought I was the perfect choice.

Because of the changes in the brains of sixteen- to nineteen-year-old girls, they are able to see the needs of those around them. They are capable of more compassion and have a genuine desire to make a difference (which we talk more about in the section on Spiritual Development). This kind of idealism is a great thing.

We see many girls in these years participate in mission trips. There is an energy, a drive, toward caring. They are idealistic in that they believe they really can make a difference—and they are right. At Daystar we have older girls help with our younger kids' camps, and they are terrific in these situations. If it weren't for the idealism of the older girls, the younger kids would miss out.

We also see this play out in the friendships of Autonomous-age girls. Girls have an intensity with each other—again, a strong drive to care. So what happens is this: if Molly, for instance, is having a hard time, Spencer will get in her car and drive to Molly's house. No family dinner, no homework is going to get in the way. Her highest call at that moment is to comfort Molly.

Unfortunately, we lose a lot of this idealism as we become adults. We continue to care but not with the same intensity. There is also a drawback to the intensity of adolescence, however. It is the "that would never happen to me" type of thinking that permeates these years.

"I can drive as fast as I want (especially if I am driving to my friend's house who is sad), and I won't get a ticket."

"It doesn't matter if I don't study for this test ... it'll be fine."

"Sure, I can finish my college applications in one week."

This is the same type of idealism that shocked the minister into hiring me (Melissa) to be a youth director when I was still a youth myself. Teens think they are almost superhuman in these years, capable of anything, and they cannot be defeated.

Some teenagers believe this to a fault. Movies often perpetuate it when they portray sixteen- to nineteen-year-olds as living in a perpetual party, with no parents anywhere to be found. Rules simply don't apply. They are fun-loving, fairly empty-headed girls (and boys) whose main priority is to spend their parents' money and learn as little as possible. In the media, at least, that is what life is for teenagers.

But not all teenagers are like that in real life. Many are quite different. We know girls who struggle deeply with the issue of integrity in these Autonomous Years. They pursue Christ and who he has called them to be with courage and honesty. They are coming to understand that they enjoy life more when their energy is directed toward a higher purpose.

SPIRITUAL DEVELOPMENT

Jessica had been to drug-and-alcohol rehab already at the age of sixteen. Her father was a minister, her mother a counselor. She had heard a lot of the "right" answers and been through a lot of the "wrong" things.

She came to Daystar when she was released from rehab. I (Sissy) counseled her for several months through the spring. She was making great progress in dealing with both her past issues and her future recovery. What she wasn't dealing with, however, was her need for God.

Her mother had told me that Jessica had been very sensitive toward the Lord in her Adventurous Years, but, somehow, in the midst of the drugs, alcohol, and life on the edge, her need for him had been eclipsed by her need for narcissistic fun.

Through that spring, however, things had started to change. Jessica was softening. I knew that God was wooing her back.

I also knew she would need more than the easy answers that satisfied her in the Adventurous Years. Our summer camps were coming up—and I felt they could be an honest, powerful, safe place for Jessica to wrestle with the Lord.

After some convincing that she would not hear platitudes or pat answers, she signed up. At the end of that camp, we asked her to help with a camp for younger kids. In one week, God had used worship and Melissa's teaching to stir her heart, he had used relationships with other kids to help her discover truth and strengthen her convictions, and he had given her a sense of purpose.

Jessica is now spending her second summer on staff with us. Her story is an inspiration to us and a reminder of what girls need in their spiritual development during these Autonomous Years:

- Teaching that stirs
- Strength of conviction
- A sense of purpose

Teaching that Stirs

In his book *The Curate's Awakening*, George Macdonald says, "Polwarth did not want to say or explain too much, for he did not want to weaken by presentation the truth which, in discovery, would have its full effect."

This statement could have been written about Autonomous-age girls. Sixteen- to nineteen-year-olds learn by discovery. They need to be invited, rather than instructed.

As we teach girls in their Discovery or Adventurous Years, we teach directly. We instruct them and feed them exactly what we want them to learn, and they receive it. Even though she may ask questions, if we tell an eight-year-old the story of creation, she believes every bit of it.

Teenagers, however, are different. As we have said, their thinking is abstract. It is more complicated and responds to teaching that reaches down into those complicated places. By nature, they question, and this questioning is a necessary part of their spiritual development.

Girls are finding their own faith in these adolescent years—rather than just the faith of their parents. They are deciding what they believe about certain issues and, more importantly, about God.

Girls from sixteen to nineteen need teachers who will let them ask tough questions—and not feel like they have to give them the answers. Point these girls toward the Bible, have them pray and write about what they believe God is saying to them, ask them more questions, and stir them to discover truth rather than hand it to them.

Questioning stretches the faith of Autonomous-age girls. It gives them a strength of conviction that will help them become women with sturdy, passionate, three-dimensional faith.

Strength of Conviction

As a junior in high school, our friend Pace decided to go to a different church than her parents. With a great deal of wisdom, her parents let her go. That time was a real turning point for Pace. She was discovering truth on her own, and her faith had that much more meaning because she was doing the choosing.

From sixteen to nineteen, girls are deciding who they want to be and what they want to believe. They are developing convictions ... values ... character. There has been some development of these things all along, but it was often more by your choice than theirs.

By the end of this stage, your daughter will be making choices on her own. You won't be there to see if she's had too much to drink or if she's wearing clothes that are inappropriate. She has to make those decisions—and now is her time to start.

As we have said, her thinking has changed. Black-and-white answers no longer suffice. These girls want to know why they shouldn't have premarital sex, why they shouldn't do drugs, or why they shouldn't steal a friend's boyfriend. They want to know the reasons behind the rules they have been taught most of their lives.

This is where the stirring comes back. It doesn't help Autonomous-age girls when we tell them why they shouldn't do something. They need to discover it on their own, and they are finally capable of doing so in these Autonomous Years. But what we can do is facilitate the process. We can give them opportunities to talk and think through what they do believe. We can help them find other groups of kids who are wrestling with the same issues, and once again, we can ask questions that help them clarify what they believe. Let us give you a picture of what this looks like in action.

I (Sissy) recently met with a group of eleventh- and twelfth-grade girls. I knew that several girls in the group were angry about choices they had made and were struggling with self-hatred—an intense anger and shame toward themselves. It would have been easy to say, "I know several of you have been feeling bad about yourselves. I want to know why and what you can do to change things."

Instead, I asked them a question: "What's the difference between self-hatred and repentance?" What these girls came up with *on their own* was that self-hatred is being stuck while repentance is moving forward. They talked about self-hatred being easier, because you can just feel sorry for yourself. My next question was, "When you're stuck and feeling bad about yourself, how do you handle it?" The answers ranged from getting really angry with their parents to pushing their friends away to not allowing themselves to eat. As the girls answered this final question, it dawned on them that these behaviors were actually sin.

It wasn't that I had great insight. I just asked two questions, and these girls, in their abstract thinking, arrived there themselves.

Girls in their Autonomous Years are capable of developing their own values and ideals. As they discover what they believe, through stirring teaching and discussions, they will develop their own strength of conviction.

A Sense of Purpose

As we were writing this book, we asked two different groups of girls, one in their Narcissistic Years and the other in their

Autonomous Years, to describe in one word how they would like to be described. These are their answers.

NARCISSISTIC YEARS	AUTONOMOUS YEARS
☆ Cool	☆ Strong-willed (but not in a bad way)
☆ Fun to be around	☆ Stands up for what I believe
☆ Smart	☆ Respected
☆ Funny	☆ Loving
☆ Considerate	☆ Original
☆ Caring	☆ Light of the Lord
☆ Perfect	☆ Unique
☆ Popular	☆ Loyal
☆ Trustworthy	☆ Selfless
☆ Not bad (in trouble at school)	☆ Purehearted
☆ Hip	☆ Beautiful (but not of looks)
☆ A best friend	☆ Magnetic
☆ Sunshine	☆ Deep and perceptive

The majority of adjectives to describe the Narcissistic-age girls have to do with how other people see them. The adjectives for the Autonomous-age girls have to do with who they are.

These sixteen- to nineteen-year-olds are becoming much of what they hope others see in them. They are purposefully becoming. And that purpose—that desire to give, to offer something of who they are, is a hopeful characteristic of Autonomous-age girls.

Girls in eleventh and twelfth grades often become bored in settings like youth group and school. We can easily see the same things happen in our groups at Daystar. Why do these girls become bored? Partly because we continue to teach them at seventeen the same way we taught them at twelve. We instruct rather than stir. The other reason is that these girls are ready—

physically, emotionally, and spiritually—to experience purpose. It is how they want to be described.

They have the ability to take someone else's perspective. They are compassionate. They can see a need in someone else and have a need themselves to give.

This has a great deal to do with our model of counseling at Daystar. It is made up of three words: *soften*, *shape*, and *strengthen*. Clay has to be softened before it can be shaped into what it is meant to become. Softening is creating a relationship with the child or adolescent that frees them to trust. Shaping is the actual teaching. Clay has to be softened before it can be shaped. After it is shaped, it is thrown in the kiln for strengthening. Without strengthening, the clay cannot be used.

For a teenage girl, finding a sense of purpose is strengthening. This occurs at Daystar as sixteen- to nineteen-year-olds help with our younger kids' groups or younger kids' camps. This helps them believe not only in themselves but that what they have been through really matters.

Last summer, a senior in high school participated in our camps for the first time. She had courageously struggled for years with an eating disorder and finally felt as though she was winning the battle. We asked this young woman to help with our seventh and eighth grade camp.

As the camp was coming to a close, she stopped both of us in the kitchen to talk to us. "I can't ever thank you enough for letting me be here. I never really believed that I would be able to see a reason for what I had been through. I never thought God could use it. But he has. He has let me talk to girls who are struggling with the same thing. I finally feel like all that I have been through can make a difference in someone else's life."

This young woman now wants to make a career out of working with girls who have eating disorders. She has found a sense of purpose—and that purpose has helped her discover more of who she is.

PARENTING DURING THE AUTONOMOUS YEARS

We have talked at length in the chapters on development about helping to call out who God is creating your daughter to be. In small ways, you will continue to do that for the rest of her life. But the loudest, most direct part of your calling is over in these Autonomous Years.

She is finding her own voice. Her body, her emotions, and her faith are working together to give your daughter the ability to care, to give, and to have a sense of purpose that is outside herself. In these years, she is discovering who she believes God is calling her to be.

What, then, does your role look like in these Autonomous Years? Mostly, it looks like a friend-size safety net. You haven't entirely left your authority behind. You are widening your daughter's boundaries so that the changes in her eighteen-year-old life will be minimal. When she falls, you are helping her get back on her own two feet. But most importantly, you are walking beside her and reinforcing with your love and support all that she is wondrously becoming.

PART TWO

What's Going On with Her

CHAPTER 6

The Longing for Relationships

[Women's] longings for relationships are relentless reminders of what we were made for and what is worth living for.

SHARON HERSH, *BRAVE HEARTS*

During our summers at camp, we take a sixteen-mile bike ride with a group of boys and another bike ride with a group of girls. The two rides couldn't be more different. The boys pedal with a sense of purpose. They are trying to reach their destination—as quickly as possible. They might joke with each other a little along the way, but mostly they are independently pushing themselves toward their goal.

The girls, on the other hand, meander. We have a long, slow, enjoyable ride. There are typically several clumps of girls deep in conversation about friendships or boys. A mile or so up the road, there is usually a group singing their favorite childhood songs at the top of their lungs. The purpose of the girls' ride is more in the relationships formed than the accomplishment of reaching the goal.

This difference is reflective of a much deeper one that exists between men and women. In his book *The Wonder of Girls*, psychologist Michael Gurian refers to what he calls the "intimacy imperative" that drives a girl's thoughts and her behaviors. According to Gurian, a boy's primary search is for independence while a girl's is for intimacy. Thus, the behavior on the bikes.

Girls want independence too, just as boys want intimacy, but that search is not the one that defines them. Think back on your own years in middle school. As a girl, to have a boyfriend in the seventh grade means you have arrived. He gives you status and security. For a boy, however, it is alternately a source of profound joy and profound embarrassment. He will be sweet to his girlfriend on the phone, but as soon as his friends come around, he ignores or makes fun of her. He wants independence. She wants intimacy.

For girls, it is this search for intimacy that provides the backdrop for the rest of life. Girls define themselves by how they connect. They have passion and purpose and heart that stretches beyond relationship—but relationship is where it stretches from. It provides the context, the framework for who girls are becoming ... for their identities.

THE IMPORTANCE OF RELATIONSHIP

In preparing to write this book, we asked girls of all ages a series of questions. The first question we asked was "What is the hardest part of being a girl?" Here is a sampling of the answers we received:

SEVEN- TO NINE-YEAR-OLDS

- other people laughing at me
- picking clothes out
- being teased by boys
- being left out
- parents yelling at you

TEN- TO ELEVEN-YEAR-OLDS

- crying
- shaving, dealing with period, doing hair
- being bullied and yelled at in school
- trying not to gossip
- keeping up with homework

TWELVE- TO FOURTEEN-YEAR-OLDS

- dealing with gossip and critical girls
- having to get the right kinds of clothes
- having to be someone you're not to fit in
- worrying about peer pressure and what other people think about you
- worrying about impressing guys
- dealing with emotions (especially at that time of the month)

FIFTEEN- TO SIXTEEN-YEAR-OLDS

- trying to fit in
- worrying about how you look
- getting caught in the middle of drama with other girls—fights, competition, overanalyzing things, gossip
- knowing if you can trust a guy or not
- dealing with periods and maturing faster or slower than your friends

SEVENTEEN- TO NINETEEN-YEAR-OLDS

- feeling like you have to look good because you're a girl
- dealing with how cruel girls are to each other
- dealing with popularity (or lack of it) and self-esteem (or lack of it)
- thinking boys will make us happy and then seeing how immature they are at our age
- dealing with emotions, especially during PMS

There are several themes that come through in the answers of these girls. Boys, popularity, clothes, and trust plague girls of all ages, but the one thing that looms in the background of most of these answers is, once again, *relationship.* Popularity is about relationship. What clothes to wear has to do with what other people think. Worrying about being talked about, or actually being talked about, has to do with relationship. Regardless of the specific subject, the root remains the same. Girls spend their time worrying about, investing their energy in, and finding their identities in relationships.

RELENTLESS REMINDERS

My (Melissa's) close friend Nita once said that relationships are the best and the worst things that happen to us. Whatever takes us to the heights of joy and the depths of sorrow most often has to do with relationships: the birth of a child or grandchild, the loss of a spouse or friend. The gains, losses, troubles, and triumphs bound up in relationships engage the heart of a woman like nothing else has the power to do.

Carol Gilligan, Michael Gurian, and Larry Crabb are three psychologists who have written at length on the differences between women and men. They describe the primary needs of each differently, with terms such as *security* and *significance*, *connection* and *independence*, and *intimacy* and *purpose*. But the bottom line of all of their research is that men and women look for fulfillment in separate ways: men in independence and purpose, and women in interdependence and care.

Men care and find value in relationship, but their search for fulfillment has primarily to do with their sense of purpose. Women want to make a difference as well. We also want independence, but for women, our relationships most engage our hearts. These relationships have the incomparable power to draw out our passions, hopes, fears, and longings. As Sharon Hersh says, they are "relentless reminders of what we were made for and what is worth living for."

As you look back over the physical development of girls from an early age, it is obvious that God hardwired women for relationship, creating them to desire and find fulfillment in connection both to others and, ultimately, to him. But it takes us about twelve years to come to this awareness.

THE DAM BREAKS

In our group counseling sessions at Daystar, we have around six girls who regularly attend second-to-fourth- and fifth-to-sixth-grade groups. In the group for seventh and eighth graders, we have fifteen. Why does this happen? Because middle school is the time when these relational longings begin to surface.

In elementary school, girls want friends. They want to have friends over, and they want to be invited to slumber parties. They even cry, at times, when they are not included. They may have "boyfriend" relationships that last about an hour at school. These girls are already experiencing and investing in relationships.

I (Sissy) counsel a precious, precocious fourth grader named Erin. As Erin and I talked during our first session, she told me about several girls in her class who had made fun of her—for her shoes (which happened to be red and green striped Converse high-top tennis shoes). We discussed the fact that these girls were most likely jealous—and they didn't feel good enough about themselves to wear anything that might be different. We talked about the fact that difference is really a good thing.

A few weeks later, the class cross-stitched Christmas gifts for their moms. Erin's mom came in to tell me about what Erin had made for her. Most of the kids did obvious things like "I love you" or "Merry Christmas." Erin, on the other hand, wisely cross-stitched the words, "Difference is beauty."

In middle school, girls often stop thinking difference is beauty. For many of them, difference becomes an embarrassment. Difference makes you stand out which makes you not look like everyone else, which makes you weird in a middle school mind. Difference can keep you from the thing that beginning in middle school takes on the very highest degree of importance—relationship.

In contrast to Erin, we recently spoke with Allison's mom. Allison is thirteen and had decided with several of her friends to participate in a walk for children in Africa. After Allison had decided to walk, she and her mom watched a television program outlining the mission of the event, and the sponsors asked each participant to write or draw a picture for their senator, to help the government have the participant's concern documented in writing.

Allison was really excited and motivated to do the walk with her friends, but when her mom told her they would be writing their senator, Allison burst into tears. "NO, MOM!!! None of my friends will be writing the senator. You just can't make me do that. You don't understand."

Her mother's wise response was, "Allison, you don't understand the point." Allison's benevolent heart was more social in its motivation than philanthropic. She wanted to be a part of the walk because her friends were, and she sure didn't want to do anything different. Her tears were tied up in her longing for relationship and her fear of looking weird.

We see a lot of girls in middle and high school struggle with depression. Much of this has to do with these longings for relationship. The dam has broken. These girls want relationship, and that wanting can be awfully uncomfortable.

PLUGGING UP HOLES

"I hate that I want. If I could get to the point where I don't want anyone to care or love me, life would be perfect."

The girl who said these words was aware of her longings. Her dam had broken—and she hated it. She did not want to long for anything ... or anyone. That is the response for many of us.

We don't want to want. God designed us to long for relationship, but we wish he didn't. Why? The answer lies in several fears that we have about ourselves in relationship. We may believe our longings are too strong—that others won't be able to handle us or our longings. We may believe our longings will get us into trouble by causing us to be too intimate in a relationship, or we may believe our longings simply won't be met. These are our fears. The reality, however, is not too far off. The truth is that, this side of heaven, our longings are very rarely met when—or in the way—we want them to be.

Another high school girl recently told us, "I would rather not feel than feel disappointment." This young girl gives to her friends in tremendous ways. She is aware of them, listens to them, and lives her life with a commitment to care for them in a way that is rare among teenage girls. But she longs for that kind of love to be returned. She was not just created to give, but also to receive, and her friends drop the ball regularly, as friends often do.

So how does this girl respond? She does what so many of us do as women. She runs back to the dam. She sticks her fingers into the fissures to try to plug up the ever-increasing holes.

Girls do this ... women do this. As soon as we realize that the dam has burst, we start trying to plug it up. Even with water pouring out all over us, we still believe there is something we can do to stop this flood of our longing hearts.

The primary ways girls try to deal with the holes are:

- Ignoring the holes—denial
- Filling the holes—addictions
- Breaking down the dam—self-hatred

Ignoring the Holes—Denial

I (Melissa) recently met with a senior in high school for the first time. This young woman had a beautiful smile and was very kind. She said all the right things as we talked, but there was a vacancy in her eyes and voice. She told me about not fitting in at school and staying home most weekends. She also said it didn't really bother her.

This young woman is ignoring the fact that there are holes in her dam. She is not allowing herself to long for more in relationship with her friends. She is not opening herself up to relationship with boys her age. She is simply taking her heart and going underground.

Many women do this. We flatten ourselves emotionally so that we don't have to be disappointed. The problem is that our joy and sorrow are linked together. As we cut off disappointment, we also cut off happiness. We can't deaden one side of our hearts without it eventually affecting the rest. Therefore, a girl or a woman who ignores holes quickly deadens emotionally. In trying to silence our longings, we silence our entire hearts.

Filling the Holes — Addictions

Another option for plugging holes is to fill them with something else. For many adolescent girls, these hole-fillers are destructive. Drugs, alcohol, eating disorders, and self-mutilation are a few of the ways that girls try to fill their longings. Rather than feeling the longing, they do something dangerous that will take their mind off the disappointment. We will talk more about these fillers in chapter 9.

This kind of longing is opening yourself up to pain. Filling the holes is another way to deaden that pain. The problem is that the holes still leak, so trying to fill them becomes even more frenetic. As we know, drugs lead to more drugs. Drinking one night a week doesn't cut it for very long. Bodies ravaged by eating disorders must get thinner and thinner to be attractive in the mind of the anorexic. With self-mutilation, the scratches have to get longer and deeper or occur more frequently.

It is as if filling holes only makes the holes deeper. These girls quickly end up on a path to self-destruction unless they get help. Their emotions are still there; they're just buried beneath a lot of self-destructive dirt.

Breaking Down the Dam — Self-Hatred

Self-hatred is an issue we see in a distressing number of teenage girls. I (Sissy) recently spoke with a girl whose boyfriend had just broken up with her. Her response is one that all of us have probably heard or said at some point in our lives: "I can't believe he did this. He doesn't even speak to me in the halls anymore. But I keep trying to get him to talk to me. I don't know why. I don't even know how to stop liking him. I'm just such an idiot!"

There is nothing idiotic about this young woman. In fact, she is doing just what God designed her to do—long for relationship. But, rather than allowing herself to be angry at her ex-boyfriend, or just sitting in the sadness of her breakup, she is angry with herself. She hates herself for longing.

It is easier to blame ourselves than feel disappointed. At least the blaming is in our control. We would rather break down the dam than watch it slowly crumble.

The danger in this approach is that self-hatred is like a black hole. We just become angrier and angrier with ourselves, and that kind of self-hatred eventually spills over onto others. These girls end up pushing people away because they won't believe they are worthy of anyone's love. Self-hatred will turn into more insecurity, more isolation, and often even depression.

We need to point out, however that there are "constructive" ways to ignore or fill holes. For a girl to immerse herself in a sport, a leadership position, or even a youth group can be an attempt to fill holes. Shopping, reading, and spending time with friends can fulfill the same purpose. The idea that these activities are viewed positively by society doesn't lessen the fact that they can also be used to fill holes.

Friendships, athletics, arts, volunteering, and academic studies are all good things—necessary things in the life of a girl. So how can you tell when they have become less of an interest and more of a hole filler? When she panics when she can't do them. If your daughter feels, like we hear many teenagers say, that she is terrified to be alone—her friends may be a hole filler. If she picks up her books every time she is sad or stressed, rather than talking about it or even letting herself cry—her studies may be a hole filler.

Your daughter needs a variety of interests and places she can give of herself. But she also needs to feel. If those activities are taking the place of her longings, you don't need to stop her from participating in the activities. But you may want to mention to her what you see happening. Ask her about it. Draw her out in a way that helps her know it is safe to feel those longings.

No matter how we do it, ignoring holes, filling them with something else, and breaking down the dam ourselves simply creates more problems. And none of these attempts at control even come close to what we truly long for.

THE DEEPEST LONGING

A book I (Sissy) read as a nineteen-year-old was *Inside Out* by Dr. Larry Crabb. That book changed everything for me. It was the first time I heard that, first, I was designed to have longings and, second, my longings would never be fully met until heaven. I read that book with a sigh of relief. To know that nothing was wrong with me for longing, that it was a part of the reality of a fallen world to be disappointed, and that God would fulfill my deepest longings was profoundly freeing for me.

Girls become aware of their longings and believe they will be met. It takes a few years, a lot of knocks, and quite a bit of maturity to realize that our fulfillment comes only in short spurts this side of heaven.

We want girls to have hope and to expect good, but not to expect perfection. To know that every relationship holds some degree of disappointment, to know that no person or job or event is going to complete them until heaven is powerfully freeing.

The only better gift is an understanding of the cross.

At a conference we attended, Sharon Hersh gave a memorable

picture of this truth. She said that our lives are much like the road to the Grand Canyon. Along the way, there are signs. Some of the signs say "247 miles to the Grand Canyon." Some say, "Grand Canyon Souvenirs 2 miles to the left." Some say, "Grand Canyon official T-shirts sold here."

These signs point us toward the canyon. But some of us get stuck at the signs. We sit down to rest or buy a T-shirt and forget where we're really headed.

She likened the signs to many of the relationships girls experience. One sign might be a sought-after group of friends. One might be marriage, another children, another a rewarding job. We love these signs. We sit under them and enjoy all that they offer. But they are signs. They are pointing us toward something much more important. If we get stuck at a sign, we will never reach the Grand Canyon.

Some of the signs along the way we may miss entirely—not having a boyfriend during high school, for example, or not having children as an adult. But when we come to the Grand Canyon and step up to that edge for the first time, all signs—stopped at or missed—will be forgotten. They will fade away in the wonder of the glorious destination.

Longings are just like signs. Girls long for relationships—with boys and then men, for children, for friendships that are lasting—and for purpose in those relationships. These longings are good and God given. He wants us to enjoy the gifts he gives us on earth, but these gifts are just a foretaste of what is to come. As the psalmist says, "As the deer longs for streams of water, so I long for you, O God" (Psalm 42:1, NLT).

Jesus meets our deepest longings—he is what we long for in our deepest parts. Our desires to be loved, to be secure, to be known, to have purpose—all these and more are met in our relationship with Christ. Our other longings are real and important. They will be a source of profound joy and pain in our lives, but they will never fulfill us in the way that our relationship with him will. This understanding is the greatest gift we can give our girls.

The cross holds the answer to every one of their and our deepest longings. There, Jesus offers us a love that will never end—a love that is unconditional. As our girls, and as we, come to understand this kind of love, we are freed to love others.

As we experience love that will not disappoint us, we are freed to be disappointed. We are free to risk, free to long. First John 4:18 says, "Perfect love drives out fear." Because we are loved perfectly, we are freed to be loved and to love imperfectly.

The dam does break. Your daughter will have longings, just as you do. But you have a great deal to offer her—spiritually and practically—to help her understand her longings and where those longings will ultimately be fulfilled.

HOW WE CAN HELP

Girls are going to crash headlong into their longings around the age of middle school—and they won't know what hit them. As a parent, you can help your daughter immensely at this time. You can help her spiritually by doing the things we talked about in the last section. You can also help her practically.

First, help her know that it's okay to want relationships and that it is okay to feel hurt in those relationships. She may not admit these things to you, but you can still talk to her about them. Show her the Psalms. Share your own stories of hurt and disappointment. Help her understand what it means to go to God with her pain.

Also, help her connect with kids who can share this kind of truth—in youth group, in school, at summer camp, in group counseling. It frees her to talk about these things as she hears other kids talk about them. It will also give her another place to know that she is loved and valued.

Next, read books and watch movies like *Anne of Green Gables* in which girls have close, meaningful friendships. Talk about these books and movies. Help her see that some of her favorite characters have longings of their own.

Finally, go on trips or out to dinner with friends regularly. Plan trips and dates with your spouse—without children. Allow her to see the importance of your own relationships.

If we do not give girls a vocabulary to talk about their longings, they will think something is wrong with them. We give them this vocabulary not only in words, but by our example.

We speak to them about Christ in the same way. Longings are "relentless reminders," as Sharon Hersh says, "of what life is worth living for and what we were made for." As girls learn to acknowledge and experience their longings, they begin to enjoy them more and look forward to their fulfillment in the unconditional love of Christ.

CHAPTER 7

Family Ties

We often speak of a family circle, but there are none too many of them. Parallel lines never meeting, squares, triangles... these and other geometrical figures abound, but circles are comparatively few.

KATE DOUGLAS WIGGIN, *MOTHER CAREY'S CHICKENS*

This chapter doesn't need much of an introduction. It is about family—with all its parallel lines, squares, and triangles included. The lines and shapes we describe are those of mom, dad, siblings, grandparents, extended family, and even pets. Not necessarily circles—just individuals God has purposefully placed in the life of a girl.

Families don't have to be perfect to make a difference. In actuality, the more the lines don't meet just right, often the more life and passion and personality that is contained within. Girls don't need perfection, they just need a group of people willing to walk alongside, love them, and help them transform into the women God is calling them to be.

THE ROLE OF MOMS

As a girl develops, her mom changes just as much as she does. She starts off as the best Band-Aid-putter-on-er and crossing-the-street-hand-holder of all times. She then becomes a pretty good carpool driver and soccer cheerleader. What seems like weeks later, she passes through a stage where she is not really good at anything and becomes much less intelligent than her daughter.

She doesn't know anything about fashion—or friends—or especially what other kids are allowed to do. Finally, she regains all her intelligence and actually knows a lot about life and relationships. It is amazing how much a mother can change in nineteen years.

Obviously, moms don't really change in these ways. In actuality, many girls feel that their moms are the most stable relationship they have—which also makes them the easiest target. What changes is not the identity of the moms but the roles they are allowed to have in the lives of their daughters.

Home Plate

During the Discovery Years, mom is home plate. She represents all that is safe and accepting in a child's life. She is the one her daughter wanders away from and comes back to—time and time again. She provides the backdrop for her daughter's exploration of life. She wanders away but wants to remain within sight of her mother's ever-watchful eye (and adoration—as we talked about in chapter 2).

This role will continue to be the foundation of a mother's relationship with her daughter. Her wandering away and coming back will continue, although it will look a little different. But, in the next few years, other aspects of their relationship will play a more predominant role.

Chauffeur

As a daughter moves into her latter elementary school years, the hours from four o'clock to seven become the busiest in the day—for girls and their moms. Moms of daughters from about ten to sixteen years of age don't have time to be home plates—they are so busy acting as chauffeurs.

Many mothers of girls in this age tell us that their very best conversations with their daughters occur in the car. In these years, girls are becoming more uncomfortable with face-to-face interaction. Herein lies the gift of practices, lessons, and plays. Girls and moms are given an environment to talk that is neutral (in that it is not home where the room needs to be cleaned), indirect (rather than face-to-face), and captive (where girls cannot escape to their computers or cell phones). In this setting moms can engage their daughters in conversations about their lives, school, and relationships—and hear things they might never hear sitting around the dining-room table. Even though they are sometimes exhausting, these are valuable years and car rides for both the girl and her chauffeur.

Foil

I (Sissy) never knew what the word *foil* meant until I became one last summer. We had a teenage girl at camp who was angry with every rule we had—and predominantly with me for being the camp director. Our friend Mimi's response was, "She just needs a foil."

A foil is much like an antagonist—the sole purpose of their existence is to make the main character look better. They stand opposite each other—at all times. Let me say that it is not fun to be a foil.

Unfortunately, this is the role of most moms as their daughters move into adolescence. If a mom says wear the pink shirt, she wears blue. If she likes her friend Brittany, she invites over Mary—and so on. The following paragraph is solely for moms:

Even though you feel like a foil right now, you are still your daughter's home plate. She loves you—deeply. But for many girls, it is in no way cool to be as close to your mom as a thirteen- or fourteen-year-old. This too shall pass. It is not personal. There will be cracks in the foil as you put her to bed some nights and have glimpses of who she used to be. She will become this girl again. Enjoy the cracks, and continue to hold true to who you are. Be silly around her. Have life. Dance in the car (as long as her friends aren't with you—that would be humiliation). But don't change who you are just because she is changing. She still needs you to be home plate, and home plate doesn't move. During her foil years, she just needs to stand opposite you to find her own identity, and that identity may temporarily take her to the deepest part of outfield.

We want to make one side-note here. There is a phenomenon we see regularly with moms and daughters that we refer to as the "hip mom factor." Basically, it is very hard for girls in these years to have moms that are ultra hip. As one adolescent girl said, "Moms are supposed to be momish ... to wear those funny-looking jeans and baggy T-shirts."

We probably wouldn't go quite this far. We believe that it is completely appropriate for moms to dress in ways that are becoming. But we do see girls struggle when their moms wear the exact same trendy jeans or tops as they do. Teenage girls often want to be the front-runners of fashion. It is a part of their identity, and a part of how they are different from their parents. My (Sissy's) mom, for example, always dressed beautifully and stylishly, but she did not wear the same clothes I did. She bought me the trendy clothes. I was allowed to be the teenager, and she the mom.

Girls do, however, love to help their moms pick out clothes. A great way to connect is to ask your daughter her opinion on what you should wear or take her with you to pick out clothes. She will feel respected and you will have an opportunity to connect in spite of your antagonistic foil-ness.

Friend

As the dust settles over the foil stage, moms reemerge as human beings in a daughter's mind. You actually are able to have a relationship again—and even have an opinion. They want to see you as more of a friend than an authority. (See chapter 5.)

Surprisingly, this is often one of the most difficult stages for moms. It involves listening more than talking. It involves letting them make their own mistakes—but helping them pick up the pieces afterward. It can involve offering advice—but mostly when they ask for it. This stage is really about letting go. As you let go of your daughter's dependence, you gain much more. To be your daughter's friend becomes one of the greatest gifts of her adulthood—for her and for you.

The Importance of Play with Moms at Every Age

It is the most natural thing in the world to play with your daughter when she is young—and often the most difficult thing as she becomes older. What comes much more naturally for moms is to instruct. "Sally, you need to take your laundry upstairs." "Please don't leave your backpack right here at the door." "You can't invite all of them without inviting Jenna." And so on and so forth. Because moms are perceptive, and sometimes simply because they are around, they are often the parent who does the most instructing of their daughters.

Girls, however, desperately need to play with their moms. It helps moms stay unpredictable and helps daughters feel more enjoyed. A friend and her three daughters dance regularly in the kitchen to Motown music. It can be dancing, enjoying a movie or a television show together, going for a bike ride, or going out for lunch.

Girls need to enjoy their moms, even when they act embarrassed to do so. Home plate is nothing if not a safe, delightful place to which to return.

THE ROLE OF DADS

In today's culture, dads are changing more diapers, coaching more teams, and spending more time with their daughters than ever before. Our friend David is just such a dad. He recently told us this story about his four-year-old daughter.

> *The kids were out of school Monday for Martin Luther King Jr. Day. We spent a good amount of time talking about the man and the reasons we celebrate his life. We read this great book about diversity and were planning to attend a march to help the kids connect with the impact of this man's life.*
>
> *Later, my daughter Lily was recalling these events with her aunt. Lily told her this was a man who taught the world that you should love people no matter what color their skin was. She went on to say that her next-door neighbor, Chelsea, has skin that looks like chocolate and our friend Miss Nicole's skin is tan like peanut butter (naturally, all of my children's analogies have to do with food). She then remarked that her own skin was white like cotton. Her aunt replied, "Lily, I love how much you understand about that. What was the man's name again who taught us that message?" Lily remarked with confidence, "John the Baptist."*

Although four-year-old Lily confused a few of the facts, she learned a very important lesson from her dad. David is a dad who understands that he has a significant role—we would say roles—to play in the life of his daughter, and he is using those roles to help call out more of who God has created Lily to be.

Playmate

Dad is often the first and best playmate a girl can have in her early years. He swings her through the air, lets her dance on his toes, and makes lots of scary noises. Dads have a natural ability to enjoy their daughters. In turn, this enjoyment helps girls feel safe in their father's care and helps them feel that they are enjoyable themselves. Thankfully, in today's culture, dads are much more present in the daily (and nightly) lives of their daughters than they have ever been. They take on a multitude of roles, but one of their best is still that of playmate.

Much like home plate with moms, being a playmate is a role that remains throughout the life of a girl with her dad. And this role is just as important as she grows older as it is in her younger years.

Coach

In their Adventurous Years, dads not only offer their daughters a sense of enjoyment but also a sense of adventure. They introduce them to new activities that require a little more courage from their daughters and often a healthy dose of interaction with dad. Dads help girls learn to take risks as they teach them to play softball, take them on hikes, and coach their basketball teams. They take them whitewater rafting and horseback riding. My (Sissy's) dad taught me to swing dance (which he called the Arkansas Push), drive a boat, and fish.

Dads have an almost uncanny ability to push their daughters toward new activities, while still enjoying them at the same time. They help daughters grow in both their confidence and their courage.

Unfortunately, for many girls, this playing and coaching comes to a dramatic halt with the onset of puberty.

The Perils of Puberty

Several years ago, a father came in for counseling. All he could talk about was what a hard time his wife was having with their thirteen-year-old daughter. He said that his wife's feelings were hurt continually by his daughter's rebuffs. The next week, the mother came in. We very compassionately asked about how things were going with her daughter. Her response was, "Oh, I'm fine. I'm tired of her attitude, but I'm fine. Her dad, however, is having a really tough time."

Actually, this happens a lot with families. As little girls outgrow (for the most part) the laps of their dads, they also grow bodies that look more like women than little girls. It happens simultaneously. The result is that dads often feel the combined loss of their daughter and discomfort with this new pubescent creature living in their home.

What sometimes follows is that the discomfort of these dads turns into painful situations with their daughters. They don't know what to do, so they tease. They tease girls about their developing bodies or about their weight. These fathers mean well and are trying to connect but end up making a girl feel worse about herself and her body.

During puberty, however, dads' roles become even more important in helping draw out a girl's femininity. She doesn't want to hold his hand anymore, but she still needs him. She needs him to help her feel valued as a woman, to show her what it looks like to respect a woman, and to continue to connect with her.

The next section is written expressly for dads:

Fathers, your daughters still need you as they reach puberty—they may even need you more now than ever before. It is a painful time to be a father. She may not look quite like the "daddy's girl" she has been—but that girl is still lurking somewhere underneath.

There are a few things specific things we believe you have to offer your daughter in this confusing time. As a man, you have a unique ability to draw out her beauty—deeper beauty—than possibly anyone else in her life. Tell her that she is beautiful. Encourage her and tell her when you see her kindness toward a friend or her tenderness toward an animal. As you do these things, you touch on the femininity that is growing inside her.

You can also continue to be affectionate with her, even when she pulls away. She will be embarrassed by this, but that is all part of the adolescent ruse. It's embarrassing for your dad to do these things. But she still enjoys them—even when she acts like she doesn't. Put your arm around her at church. Offer her your arm when you are walking into an event. This kind of affection helps her feel cared for and valued.

Your daughter will look to you to determine what kind of man she wants to marry and what a marriage relationship should look like. If you are married, she needs to see you value her mother. To see you care for her not only helps your daughter understand what a loving relationship looks like, it also helps her feel more secure.

As she moves into puberty, it will be harder to find ways to connect with her. Please don't stop trying. Teach her to dance. Take her rock-climbing if she has outgrown some of the other adventurous activities you have shared. Take her shopping or out to dinner by yourselves. As she gets older, teach her to drive a car. Girls tell us they love to drive with their dads. Wash the car with her. You can also teach her to change a flat tire. There are many ways to connect with older girls; they just require a little more creativity. Remember that your daughter's distance is not a rejection of you but an absorption with herself that characterizes the Narcissistic Years. She is still daddy's girl—it's just buried beneath a lot of makeup and hair products!

Sounding Board

As girls pull away from their mothers, they often move toward their dads. This is helpful for girls in that they are learning to see themselves as separate from their mothers and they are able to align themselves a little more with their fathers. Girls need a sounding board—another person they can go to when "Mom is being totally unfair" or "she doesn't understand my life at all!" Girls will definitely have these moments. As they do, dads are able to listen and gently point girls back toward both the reality of the situation and relationship with their moms.

A dad's role as sounding board, however, can also be destructive. We know a woman who, as a young teenager, struggled in all the typical ways with her mom. When she was upset, she would run to her dad. His response was, "I know your mom can be really unfair. She makes me feel that way too sometimes."

The result was that her attitude toward her mother became even worse. She aligned herself too much with her dad. She sank to his level, and the mother became more like the problem child. This gave the girl too much power and eroded any respect she might have had for her mother.

To be a positive sounding board, her dad could have said something more like, "Honey, I'm so sorry you're hurt. I know things feel awful right now." Long pause. "What do you think your mother was really saying to you? Are you sure she doesn't understand you at all? Why don't we think of some things your mom does to try to understand you better?"

In the second example, the father is still listening to his daughter. He hears her perspective but also knows that her perspective is one of a child. He is bringing her back to the truth about her mom.

Fathers and mothers will disagree. Girls have a mysterious ability to find these cracks and use them. They actually learn quickly to manipulate their fathers. Even when you disagree as parents, girls need to see you as a unified front. Back each other up, and then disagree behind closed doors, and away from young ears and eyes.

Disciplinarian

Behold, I send you out as sheep in the midst of wolves. Therefore be wise as serpents and harmless as doves.

Matthew 10:16 NKJV

In our book *The Back Door to Your Teen's Heart*, Matthew 10:16 is one of the primary verses we talk about in parenting adolescents. It also holds true for other ages. Parents need the wisdom of a serpent—shrewd, aware, with a little bit of fearfulness mixed in—and the gentleness of a dove—kindness, compassion, and tenderness.

What happens all too often, however, is that one parent takes on the role of a dove while the other becomes the serpent. You can imagine how a girl would feel about her snake parent in contrast to her dove parent. It all plays out in a good-cop-versus-bad-cop scenario. Although the police force may at times use this tactic, we don't believe it is the most effective parenting technique.

Girls need each parent to be both gentle and wise, but often, during adolescence, fathers need to carry a little more of the serpent side. Girls and their moms naturally struggle in their teenage years. The mom takes on the role of bad cop—just because she is often the one who sees see the clothes left out and who gets the brunt of her daughter's attitude. In these situations, we tell the fathers it is helpful not only to his wife but also to his daughter for him to be more of the disciplinarian.

Girls need and truly long for their fathers to have strength with them—strength mixed with compassion. This helps them feel safe, cared for, and ultimately helps them see God as a father who is both strong and caring on their behalf.

We do want to say that girls who don't have a relationship with their father can still learn these truths about men and about God. If your ex-husband or husband is not involved in the life of your daughter, help her connect in places where she can have safe, encouraging relationships with men: youth directors, camp counselors, and teachers are great examples. Uncles, grandfathers, and close friends are also able to step in and fill an important role. Ultimately, God knows what and whom your daughter needs in her life. And death, divorce, or neglectful mothers or fathers will not impede his love for your daughter in any way.

THE ROLES OF SIBLINGS

Girls of all ages tell us that one of the most frustrating aspects of their lives are their siblings. The reasons primarily have to do with age—little brothers and sisters are "annoying," while older brothers and sisters "don't want me around." Regardless of age or gender, siblings can, at times, appear to be the bane of your daughter's existence.

We know the truth, however. As a high school girl recently told us, "My brother and I fight all the time, but secretly we love each other."

Siblings have this kind of ability—to double as each other's outlet for every shred of frustration and at the same time be the other's most ardent defender. We have girls say to us frequently, "I can say that to my sister [or brother], but no one else can." This is because, through all of the shoving and arguing in the back seat, they truly care for each other.

Siblings have a positive effect on the life of a girl, with a unique ability to help build her confidence and discover her identity.

Building Confidence

We often think of confidence being built by success and encouragement, but it is also built by scrapes and scuffles. Last summer I (Melissa) taught the girls at camp about a word many of them had never heard—*moxie*. *Moxie* is defined as "courage combined with inventiveness"—and not much builds moxie in a girl's life better than brothers and sisters.

As she fights with her sister for room to talk around the dinner table, she develops courage. As she tries to outsmart her brother to get the keys to the car, she develops inventiveness. Courage and inventiveness help her learn to stand up for herself. As she argues with them (to a healthy degree), she learns to stand up for what she wants and what she believes is important, and as she does so, she also discovers more of who she is.

Discovering Identity

If your oldest child is an athlete, your next child will often be an artist. If your middle child is strong academically, your youngest child will probably be more of a social butterfly. Girls like to be individuals—not replicas of their siblings. This doesn't mean you won't have two artists or athletes in the family, but for the most part, siblings want to shine in their own ways and have their own identities.

In my (Melissa's) family, one child is a writer, one a doctor, and the other a counselor. My (Sissy's) family is more of the exception to the rule. My sister and I are uncannily similar—which is because there are sixteen years between us. We are more like two only-children. The age difference between siblings does affect this choosing of roles.

Siblings create a natural, healthy competition in families as girls learn to find different areas in which to excel. They help girls learn to share, to defend themselves, and even take more risks. It is important, however, for parents to be aware of the degree of defending and risk-taking going on among siblings.

While it can be helpful for girls and their siblings to learn to work through issues without a parent always stepping in to rescue, this working through can become destructive at times. If one of your children becomes too physical, or a child makes damaging comments to another, it is definitely time to intervene. Siblings have a great deal to offer each other as they grow together, but since they are still children, they will sometimes need your help to see what it means to grow with each other rather than tear each other down.

THE ROLE OF GRANDPARENTS

Grandparents are a tremendous gift in the life of a girl. We both have very fond memories of our grandparents. My (Melissa's) grandparents taught me about faith, food, and the strength of women. My (Sissy's) grandparents have taught me to enjoy life and what it means to be a woman of character.

We see more and more grandparents who are courageously raising their grandchildren in lieu of their birth parents, but for the most part, grandparents get to enjoy the benefits of their grandchildren without all the tediousness of discipline. Because of this, grandparents are able to be gifts of strength, safety, and delight in the life of your daughter.

The Gift of Strength

A friend recently told us that, growing up, she thought her grandmother was "the stuff" (the best). She loved to be around her and respected her deeply. As a senior in high school, when one of her close friends got in trouble, this friend went to her grandmother. "My best friend told me she was pregnant. I had no idea what to do or say. I knew I couldn't tell my mom—she would be really upset. So I went to my grandmother. I asked her what I should say to my friend. She told me I didn't need to say anything. I needed to find out where her doctor was and drive her."

This friend continues to do that kind of thing. She is a person who responds to a need with action and with strength, and it is a gift she learned from her grandmother.

There are times children don't feel they can talk to their parents. To have a grandparent who will listen and offer wisdom is of tremendous value to a girl.

The Gift of Safety

> *"The role that my grandparents played in my life was invaluable! Their home served as another sanctuary for me."*

Girls need safe places other than home. When a daughter is sad, sometimes the best thing in the world is for her to spend the night with her grandparents and be embraced by love, warmth, and a home-cooked meal. When she is angry with one of her parents, her grandmother can add a little humor and help her understand a little more of the parent's humanness (without eroding her respect).

Of course, not all grandparents are safe. Some are adjusting to their aging or their own life issues that prevent them from being a safe outlet for their granddaughters. But if there is a grandparent available who can offer stability and kindness, warmth and compassion, and a home a granddaughter can retreat to, then that girl has access to a ready sense of safety and connection that is of profound importance.

The Gift of Delight

I (Sissy) never heard my grandmother call me by my name. Instead, my entire life, until she died when I was thirty years old, she called me "Sugar Babe." This was a gift of delight to me.

I (Melissa) remember a time in college that I spoke to a group of students. Both my grandmothers were in town, and both came to hear me. Afterward, they didn't say a lot—but enough for me to know they were proud.

Recently our counseling ministry was trying to purchase a house for our new offices. To do so, we had to have the zoning changed from residential to commercial, and before this zoning could change, we had to meet with a group of angry neighbors—most of whom were involved in one way or another with a neighboring university.

As often happens, the kids at Daystar quickly got involved. One of the girls came to us and said, "Look, my grandfather was on the board of that school for many years. I'll call him. I know he will come to that meeting and fight for you if I ask him. He would do anything for me."

Many granddaughters we know make these kinds of comments about their grandparents. They will tell us that their grandparents adore them or think they can do no wrong. As they say these words, they often roll their eyes, but "grandparent eye-rolling" is entirely different from a "parent eye-rolling"—it's always accompanied by a smile.

Grandparents elicit this kind of response from girls. As grandparents enjoy and delight in their granddaughter, she will often act embarrassed. But the grandparents' enjoyment of her helps her to feel that she is enjoyable. She loves the fact that they love her and delight in her—and she needs them to.

THE ROLE OF PETS

We could write an entire book on this subject. In fact, as we write today, we are surrounded by Sissy's thirteen-year-old Maltese, Noel, and Melissa's nine-year-old old English sheepdog, Molasses, and an eleven-year-old cat, Patty. Both dogs are a part of our counseling ministry. We firmly believe in the power of pets in the life of a girl (and in our own lives).

Actually, I (Sissy) have told many families in the middle of a divorce that their daughters need a pet. In my own life, this is when I received Noel—as my parents were getting divorced. She has been a friend who has loved me unconditionally, taught me about responsibility, and evoked a great deal of tenderness.

Unconditional Love

God gave every pet owner a delightful surprise in the tail of a dog (even though Molasses moves her bottom since she has no tail). That tail wags—when you speak, when you smile, when you enter the room. It is a communicator of love that knows no bounds, and this kind of love does immeasurable good for a girl.

Girls can be ruthless. They can be fickle and inconsistent in their relationships, and at some point, every girl has felt or will feel the sting from these kinds of friendships.

So, for your daughter to come home from school after a particularly painful day and be greeted by a tail-wagging, licking, barking dog is like a balm to her soul. Other animals can offer the same kind of regard. But whether the pet is canine, feline, or any other kind, it is invaluable for your daughter to have a faithful source of unconditional love.

Responsibility

Responsibility is the most obvious aspect of a pet's role in the life of a girl. Pets require time and attention, and many girls fall in love with an animal before they are able to think through everything that this love entails.

For your daughter to help take care of a family pet helps her learn responsibility. It may be that a pet is a privilege as she shows you she can be responsible, but as she helps to care for a pet, she learns what caring is and thereby she endears the animal toward her even more.

Tenderness

As girls reach adolescence, they may have difficulty expressing tenderness. They may become uncomfortable with affection from their parents. They can be awkward and shy away, but even with the toughest girls, pets have an ability to draw out tenderness.

Girls who won't talk to their parents will talk to their cat. Girls will want their dog to sleep with them or cuddle when they are sad. It doesn't matter if it's a hedgehog (we actually know a girl who has one), a fish, a bird, or a cat or dog, pets provide girls with something to nurture, and this nurturing helps girls stay in touch with an important part of themselves as they disappear into the callousness and coolness of adolescence.

We hear a lot of girls talk about how painful it was to lose a pet. Even in loss, pets continue to teach girls about love. But the fact that they go back to this event shows the significance pets have in the life of a girl—a significance that brings out her care and helps her to feel cared for as she navigates the perils of growing up.

THE ROLE OF EXTENDED FAMILY

I (Sissy) met with a mom of a fourteen-year-old girl. "How long do girls stay in counseling here?" she asked.

"Well, it depends. Some girls work through their issue after several months of individual counseling, and then we have some who come, connect with a group, and stay for several years. But that is not to say that you have to be involved for a long time. It is more about what you and she need."

"Well, we need the long haul. I want someone to be in her life—and in mine to help me until she goes off to college. I can't do this by myself."

This mom explained the role of extended family in one short conversation. Extended family members can be aunts, uncles, godparents, friends who are like family, counselors, youth directors, fellow church members—anyone you choose and trust to be involved in the life of your daughter over time.

Like grandparents, extended family members have another voice—one that can speak into the life of a daughter and a parent.

Another Voice for Her

Girls don't listen to counselors like us because we've been to graduate school or because they consider us experts. Girls listen to us simply because we are a new voice.

Our voices have not been telling them for years to clean up their rooms or come in at curfew. We appear on the scene with the sole jobs of encouraging and challenging the girls who come into our offices. And then we send them home.

In fact, we often tell these girls the very same things their parents do, but because we are a new voice, these girls hear us.

As a parent, you want and need other voices speaking into the lives of your girls. These other voices can both encourage and confront your daughters ... in ways that girls often won't allow you to do. Extended family helps reinforce the traits and beliefs that you are trying to build into your daughter's life—and extended family can discourage the negative traits and beliefs as well.

Girls need and will choose other voices as they grow older. They will choose other adults to be like, who they will give power to speak into their lives. Especially as your daughter moves into adolescence, she begins to see her identity as separate from yours, and connecting with other adults helps her to do so.

Another Voice for You

Girls need other voices—as do parents. You don't need another voice because you don't know enough, but because you are living in the middle of life with your daughter.

Because extended family members are not living in your home and parenting your daughter, they can have an objective viewpoint. To ask your sister or mother or friend for help is not to admit parenting failure. It is to say that you can't see the forest for the trees.

Other voices can help you know when you're being too much of a serpent or a dove parent. Other voices can help you set parameters on bedtime and curfews. They can help you see when your frustration with your daughter has more to do with you than it does her.

Basically, to have other voices in your life can help you step back from your parenting fears and into a more confident, sensible place. They can help you be responsive ... rather than reactive. Don't be afraid to ask for help. It will help free you to be more of yourself so that you can help your daughter discover herself.

Moms, dads, siblings, grandparents, pets, and extended family all play an important role in the life of your daughter. They are your team ... and they are her coaches, cheerleaders, and fans as she becomes more of who God is creating her to be.

CHAPTER 8

Girl-Boy-Girl-Boy

"Marilla," she demanded presently, "do you think I shall ever have a bosom friend in Avonlea?"

"A–a what kind of friend?"

"A bosom friend—an intimate friend, you know—a really kindred spirit to whom I can confide my inmost soul. I've dreamed of meeting her all my life."

L. M. Montgomery, *Anne of Green Gables*

Girl-boy-girl-boy.

This is not just a seating chart for a dinner party. It is also what goes on inside a girl's brain as she grows up. A young woman recently told us that she had spent the first half of her life focused on a significant other—whether that other was a best friend or a boyfriend, it didn't really matter. She went back and forth, from one girlfriend to a boyfriend, from another girlfriend to another boyfriend—as long as she had a kindred spirit, someone who offered her a place to belong.

These kinds of relationships are important—vital to the life of a girl. She wants to belong. She wants a place—people to call her own, other than her family. Those people can be friends or boyfriends, and will probably be both.

Relationships with girls and with boys are something your daughter needs as she grows up. They are milestones that help her become. But within these milestones there are inherent rewards and risks. Our hope in this chapter is to give a little perspective on both, and to give you some practical insight as to what helps and what doesn't help your daughter as she navigates these rocky relational waters.

THE REWARDS OF FRIENDSHIP WITH GIRLS

The rewards of friendship could fill an entire book—they have, in fact, filled many. Friends help your daughter learn characteristics such as loyalty and compassion. They help her discover who she is and how she relates to others. Friends are her first, nonfamilial opportunity to learn what it means to give and receive love.

In this section, we focus on three aspects of friendship that help draw out more of who your daughter is and help her feel freer to let that person emerge:

- security
- influence
- expression

Security

Marion, a junior in high school who is involved at Daystar, went to homecoming on a blind date. It was not her own school's homecoming, although hers was on the same night. They had a nice dinner with friends and went to the dance. Several minutes after arriving, her date disappeared. When she finally found him close to half an hour later, he was dancing—rather inappropriately with his most recent ex-girlfriend. Marion was devastated. She went to her friend Amy and told her she wanted to leave but only after she told the boy exactly why she would not be going home with him.

These are Marion's words of what followed: "I went to the car and drove straight home. I cried for a few minutes before I decided that this was crazy. It was homecoming, and I didn't care about that guy anyway. I had a group of friends who were having fun at my homecoming. I knew I could go, find them, and be okay."

So Marion courageously drove herself to her own homecoming dance. She went in, found her friends, and freely danced the night away.

This is a picture of security. Marion had a hurtful experience with her first homecoming date, so she returned to a place she knew she belonged: her own group of friends.

Boys can be mean and hurtful. Girls frequently are mean and hurtful. A girl needs a place to feel secure, a place where she can go and know that she will be accepted.

Your daughter may already have this in her group of friends at school, or she may be shy and have difficulty establishing these kinds of friendships. If she does, you may need to help her. Take her to youth group, get her involved in a team sport, help her find a school club where she can find a group who will offer her security. Such a group will free her to be more who she was meant to be—to enjoy herself—and to experience fewer of the insecurities that characterize adolescence.

Influence

I (Melissa) started Daystar over twenty years ago on the premise that kids impact kids. I still believe this to be true. They hear each other's voices much louder than they ever hear ours as adults. In group counseling, I can say the same thing—many times over—but if one of their friends says it, they are shocked and amazed at their friend's wisdom.

As a parent, you can use this truth to your advantage. Your child will be influenced by her peers—for good or for not so good. You can help her find a school club where she can meet a group that will offer her security.

I (Sissy) tell parents often that the reasons girls don't get into trouble is either that (1) they have a relationship with God that keeps them from it; (2) they have a group of friends who aren't doing it; or (3) they are afraid of being punished. Sometimes it's all three, but many times it's just one.

I (Sissy, again) was a pretty "good" kid in high school. Much of the reason had to do with my group of friends. We were committed *together* to doing what we thought was the right thing (although we didn't always do it). That kind of commitment—the *together* kind—helps girls handle peer pressure much more than a parent's encouragement or even the threat of grounding.

Again, help your daughter find a place to connect, if she doesn't already have one, and if you see her connecting with girls that might not be such positive influences, help her find the more positive ones. It may be difficult, but don't give up searching. They are out there—it's just a matter of looking in the right places.

Caroline is the only girl in her group of friends at school who doesn't drink. She has strength and courage to hold true to what she believes, but she also has a group of girls she meets with every Thursday night who encourage her.

Expression

Sixteen-year-old Paige is painfully shy. She does her best to disappear in any peer group situation, and it often works. Because she is so quiet, Paige lives with a lot bottled up inside of her.

Paige's eighteen-year-old brother is a terror. He rages around her home constantly. He makes life difficult for her parents at every turn. He yells, throws things, and is hateful to Paige.

Paige has never said a word against her brother. On one hand, her parents are worried that Charles's behavior has hurt Paige. On the other, they are afraid that Paige thinks that all older brothers act this way.

So her parents brought her to Daystar and, much to Paige's dismay, put her in a group. One evening, the group got on the subject of siblings. It just so happened that several of the girls had older siblings who were difficult.

As girl after girl talked about the anger in their homes, their concern for their parents, and their loyalty to their brothers and sisters, tension drained from Paige's face.

"That's exactly like Charles. I never knew what to say about it. I hate that he hurts my mom and dad, but he's my brother. I can't help but love him."

Because these girls could understand Paige's situation, she felt free to talk, and they put words to the pain and confusion that had been ruminating inside her for years. They helped her express what she couldn't on her own.

This doesn't just happen in Daystar groups. There are groups in schools and churches in which girls are having opportunities to talk about things that are difficult.

Expression, influence, and security are three of the most important rewards that a group of friends can offer a girl. They help her become. They free her to be more of who God is creating her to be.

THE RISKS OF FRIENDSHIPS WITH GIRLS

As my (Melissa's) friend said, relationships are the best and the worst things that happen to us. Relationships will be a source of much of your daughter's greatest joy and greatest pain.

Now let's look at three risks of friendships—three areas in which girls struggle that can cause significant pain in the life of your daughter:

- mean girls
- dependent friendships
- homosexuality

Mean Girls

The movies *13 Going on 30* and *Mean Girls* both give poignant pictures of what life is like for many girls growing up today. As a matter of fact, I (Sissy) had a teenager tell me to see *Mean Girls* because she said, "That's my life."

As adults, we watch those movies and think, "This is horrible. Surely my daughter won't go through this." She may not to that degree, but she will go through some type of tyranny from other girls between the ages of ten and sixteen.

What do you do? How can you prevent it from happening? The first rule of thumb is that you can't. The only way to prevent your daughter from being hurt by other girls is to keep her from other girls.

So what are other options? Thankfully, many schools are becoming aware of the perils of girls' relationships. An elementary school in Nashville is having banquets where they create knights and princesses who have committed not to bully others. School counselors are meeting with groups of girls to help them work through issues and develop compassion. Culturally, we are reaping positive benefits of the media portrayal of girls' friendships.

Unfortunately, despite prevention and education, girls will most likely still be mean. Your daughter will still be hurt. This is where we return to your role. Give her a safe place to come home where she feels unconditionally liked and loved. When she can't say it with words, watch for signs that she is hurting: stomachaches before school, shyness around certain kids, headaches after church.

A mom of a teenager told me (Sissy): "I can always tell when Carrie is not getting along with one of her friends. She is a terror at home." Whether her signs are physical or emotional, she will tell you without telling you. Ask her questions. Give her opportunities to tell you about it, and the time to do so. Don't force her, but invite her to talk.

Let her try to handle it on her own first—but if the situation continues to escalate, step in. Then call the teacher, the school counselor, or whatever adult is in a position to help.

Your daughter will hit bumps with girls. Some of these bumps will cause you to panic; some will make you want to strangle other children. But your daughter will come through. Help her understand that mean girls are really just insecure, jealous girls, and she must be a pretty great person to bring out this much jealousy.

Dependent Relationships

> *Lonesomeness is often experienced on a very deep and painful level by adolescents and young adults. The tendency exists to look for a solution to this problem by establishing very demanding and often exhausting friendships.*
>
> HENRI NOUWEN, *INTIMACY*

A senior in high school told her group about a friendship that was much as Henri Nouwen described—exhausting, demanding, and clingy. As she talked, I (Sissy) watched other girls in the room connect with her story. I asked the girls, all of whom were juniors and seniors in high school, how many of them had been in this kind of dependent friendship. Every one of them raised their hand.

Not only will girls be mean, but they will also be intense in their relationships. Girls and women often confuse intimacy with intensity. What this means is that girls get in four-hour phone calls where one of them is in tears. Your daughter may tell you that you have to take her to her friend's house immediately because she is upset. You will watch her be an emotional drain on other girls or other girls be a drain on her.

This is a part of the evolution of the friendship of girls. I (Melissa) met with a frightened mom of a teenage girl. She described the way her daughter, Emily, acts with her best friend. "She is over at our house constantly. She stays for dinner and spends the night. They want to be together all the time. When they are together, they whisper continually. The other night, they were sitting right next to each other on the couch under a blanket."

This mother was concerned that her daughter was involved in a homosexual relationship. She was not. In fact, she was acting as many of you have probably seen your daughters do. Girls are affectionate. They are clingy and do not want to be lonesome—and so they often try to fill any emptiness with relationships. This is the nature of girls.

As the girls in the group talked about their dependent relationships, I asked them what they would have done if their parents had tried to prevent the friendships. Every one of them said that it would have pushed them toward that friend, rather than away. According to these girls, they had to learn from an unhealthy relationship what one was. They had to experience it on their own. Every one of the girls had addressed the unhealthiness and changed it on their own, as well.

This isn't always the case. Your daughter may be too much of a pleaser to get herself out of a bad situation. But as long as she is old enough, let her try first. In a back-door manner (see chapter 5), ask her what she thinks is happening between her and her friend. Ask her if there are things that make her uncomfortable. Get her to tell you what she can do about it, and then let her try. If she can't handle it, you may need to help.

If your daughter is in middle school or early high school, however, you may need to intervene sooner. Talk to her about it. Help her understand your concerns about the relationship, and then you may have to take steps to end the friendship yourself.

Homosexuality

The media has saturated our homes with portrayals of homosexuality. Almost every primetime television show has a person who is living a homosexual lifestyle. We see this impacting the social lives of girls.

In previous generations, girls had heroes. They had older girls they respected and looked up to and even emulated in the way they acted. This was a normal part of growing up. Today, it has become twisted.

If a girl feels strongly about an older girl or woman, she may unconsciously absorb the messages from television and think her feelings hint at homosexuality. If she feels quite strongly—or if she deeply cares for her best friend—she even may believe that she is gay. We believe this is a tragic result of today's media.

Girls who are clearly not homosexual often believe that they are. We have seen girls who are passionate people and care deeply about their friends truly believe something is wrong in what they feel, and then those feelings sometimes become sexualized. This is a travesty. As we have discussed throughout this book, girls deeply desire and thrive in relationship. This includes relationships with other girls.

Many of the girls we have seen in the last few years who believe they are struggling with homosexuality need simply to be told that what they long for—deep, caring relationships with friends of the same sex—is normal. But there are those who have genuinely struggled with homosexual tendencies. These girls need help from you as their parent, rather than panic.

In our offices we have seen both types of girls. We'll give you a picture of what and how each struggled with their sexuality.

Mary came into our offices because a friend told her she needed help. Mary was passionate about everything in her life—her friends, her faith, her school, and her boyfriend—and Mary had found herself in the middle of an intense, homosexual relationship with her best friend. She was also in the middle of an intense sexual relationship with her boyfriend. As Mary talked, I (Melissa) realized that what Mary was trying to do was categorize and sexualize her feelings. She was trying to make them make sense. One was sexual, and so the other must be also.

Mary told me about other women whom she respected that she had feelings for in the past. Mary's feelings were not homosexual. They were strong feelings of connection and admiration that she had sexualized because her sexuality was a predominant part of her life.

Today, Mary is still a passionate young woman. Her sexuality and her desire to connect deeply were a source of confusion for a time, but it was more as if she wandered into a homosexual relationship than purposefully walked into it.

Elizabeth, on the other hand, entered into a homosexual relationship from an entirely different perspective. Like Mary, she was a passionate, sexual young woman. Everyone she loved, she loved deeply. But Elizabeth had lost her mom to a long, hard battle with cancer at the age of five. Her mother had been sick for all of Elizabeth's life. Because her father was not around, she had grown up with her uncle and step-aunt. For as long as she could remember, Elizabeth had struggled with her femininity and her overwhelming desire to be cared for.

Elizabeth didn't wander into a homosexual relationship, as Mary had. She was purposefully looking for something. She was trying to find another female to take care of her—and to give her the affection her mother was unable to.

If, like Mary or Elizabeth, you feel that your daughter might be struggling with her sexuality, talk to her. Help her understand that you love her—*no matter what*— then take her to talk to someone, though you might want to talk to that person first. Find out where they stand on this issue emotionally and spiritually before you allow them to influence your daughter.

Girls are *becoming*. They are establishing their identity—trying to figure out who they are. Their sexuality is an important part of that identity. Your daughter will develop intense relationships as she becomes. Her longings for connection will be strong, and she will make mistakes. Whatever kind of mistakes she makes, however, there is hope for your daughter to have intimate, healthy friendships with women and relationships with men. As she comes to understand who God is and his love for her, she will better understand herself and the kind of relationships she has been created to enjoy.

THE REWARDS OF RELATIONSHIPS WITH BOYS

Much has been discussed in recent years about dating, courtship, and kissing—and when girls should do each. We are not going to decide this for parents. At your local bookstore you will find great books on these topics written by wise guides. What we want to do, instead, is to step back for a wider view—a look at the risks and rewards that boys bring into the lives of girls.

After a class I (Sissy) taught on girls, a father ran up to me saying "Boys—boys—you haven't talked enough about boys!" Fathers are frequently wary of the potential danger of boys in their daughters' lives. So if you are a dad, you might read the title of this section and say "Rewards of relationships with boys? There are none!" But give us a little time, and we'll help you understand how even boys play an important role in helping your daughter become more of who God is creating her to be.

Socialization

From time to time, girls in our groups will talk about boys. When they do (which is actually, on average, every week), there are girls who feel a little too comfortable in this arena and girls who are at a total loss. Eventually one of the more uncomfortable girls will say, "I can't imagine having a relationship with a boy. I don't even know how to talk to them. When I get around a guy, I get nervous and say stupid things."

She needs socialization. She needs safe, casual relationships with boys to help her feel comfortable. This can happen in an educational setting, but what typically happens in school is that the comfortable girls get more comfortable and the quieter girls fade into the woodwork.

For a girl to have a friendship with a boy helps boys become not quite so foreign. She learns more about who they are and how they think and how to have conversations with them. Basically, she learns to enjoy boys rather than to be afraid of them.

Now, fathers, you are saying, "Yes, and she'll learn to enjoy them too much." That's a valid concern, but, it can be equally concerning if your daughter doesn't feel that she can be herself in a relationship with a boy. You want her to feel comfortable—to be able to express who she is, what she wants, and what she doesn't want in relationship. Socialization helps her do this.

To have friendships with the opposite sex also helps girls and boys see each other as people rather than objects. Girls will sometimes say, "I want a boyfriend," when it is more about the title than it is about the person. Boys will want a girlfriend for the benefits that come with her, rather than to know her and spend time with her. As they get to know each other as friends, the playing field is leveled, and they are able to relate to each other less out of fear and more out of choice.

The Ability to Choose

As girls become comfortable around boys, they develop closer relationships. The up side of this is that they begin to see differences in guys. They see guys who are strong, guys who have depth, guys who are adventurous, and guys who are creative, and as they see these different characteristics, they begin to value certain traits over others.

Karen dated several guys in high school before she met Will. Will went to the same Christian camp and caught Karen's eye. He was athletic, fun, a gentleman, and he was the first Christian guy that Karen had ever gotten to know.

Will and Karen began a relationship that lasted several months long distance, before they lost touch with each other. But in that short period of time, Karen discovered something that is now crucial to her relationships with boys: "Now that I know how I can be treated, I'm not going to accept anything less. I also know how important it is to be able to talk to my boyfriend about God. For him to know me, he has to know that part of me."

Will also helped Karen in ways that neither of them were aware of at the time. Because of the way he treated her, Karen learned more of what it means to receive in relationship to a guy. He brought out her femininity in the little ways as he opened doors for her and in bigger ways as he pursued relationship with her.

Gradual Introduction to the World of Boys

In chapter 6, we talked about the freedoms and the dangers that come as girls move out of their parents' homes. If a girl has no prior experience with boys, casual or otherwise, this danger can be compounded. Now she doesn't have a curfew to meet, she doesn't have anyone around to monitor that the boy goes home when he should, and she is free to make her own decisions.

It is helpful for her to have already had practice in this kind of decision making while she still lives under your roof. We often tell parents the best time for girls to make mistakes is while they are at home. As she grows up, you can gradually widen the boundaries—giving her room to make her own decisions within the care of your watchful eye.

Relationships with boys follow the same principle. You want her to have enough freedom at home to be able to learn to make wise decisions regarding boys so that when she leaves home she can take that wisdom with her. Rather than completely sheltering her from situations in which she has to make good decisions, you want her to learn to make those relational decisions while she is still living with you. That way she will still make them when she's on her own.

Hannah came to Daystar because she had gotten into trouble on a school retreat for having sex. This was a shock to everyone who knew Hannah. Hannah was kind, responsible, and made good decisions—or so it seemed.

I (Melissa) saw Hannah for counseling. Hannah regularly made deep, insightful comments—even after the incident at the retreat. Like everyone else, I was impressed with Hannah's maturity and perspective.

But then, I met Hannah's mom. She is a wise, insightful woman who pursues integrity in her relationships with others and with Christ. But the things she said to me about the situation were the exact things Hannah had said to me thirty minutes earlier. I realized Hannah was not necessarily insightful. She was good at memorizing. She was mimicking everything her mother had told her about the situation. She had knowledge, but that knowledge had not seeped down into who Hannah was.

What Hannah really needed from her insightful mom was silence. As a junior in high school, Hannah needed to learn her own lessons, and face her own consequences. She was not learning to connect the dots because her mom was connecting them for her.

So when Hannah was away from home and pressured by a boy on a retreat, she had no idea what to do. Her mother wasn't there to tell her.

Hannah needed a gradual introduction to the world of boys. She needed to develop the skills on her own—to slowly learn to make good decisions with boys. She needed to see the consequences of her actions by experiencing them, not just by her mother telling her. This would have helped to minimize the risks she ran into in her relationships with boys.

THE RISKS OF RELATIONSHIPS WITH BOYS

The loneliness that propels girls into unhealthy relationships with other girls often propels them into unhealthy relationships with guys. Guys offer girls a place to belong—and that place is often one that makes her feel attractive, secure, and special in a way she has wanted for a long, long time.

The Fairy Tale Fable

As we were preparing to teach a class, we watched several movies based on fairy tales. In these, an amazing number of women (and mermaids) give up their identities—their families, homes, and fins—to be with the boy they love. Time and time again, finding the "one" is portrayed as the ultimate fulfillment of a girl's and a guy's life.

Girls fall for this fable every time. Beginning at an early age, girls dress up like brides and dream about finding the love of their life. There is a part of this fable that is good. It appeals to that part of a girl's soul that longs to receive—to be pursued. And let's face it, you *want* your daughter to require some degree of "princess treatment" from her future husband. The seeds are also being planted for her understanding of the symbolism of Christ as bridegroom and the church as the bride.

But the danger in the fable is that this fantasy world reaches its completion in romance. The movie ends, and happily ever after comes when the girl finds her true love.

We know a father who understands the fairy tale phenomenon. He tells an alternative version to his three-year-old daughter that ends something like this: "Cinderella and the Prince courted for a year and became very good friends. Then they married. They lived a very simple life and worked for social-justice issues to end the oppression of the poor. They didn't live happily ever after, but they did learn to love each other deeply ..." He also tells her how Cinderella traded in her glass slippers for hiking boots so that she and the Prince could hike all over the country.

The creativity of this father is bestowing a tremendous gift on his daughter. He is introducing her to fables and to fantasies—

and also to realities. Her happy ending will not take place as she meets the prince, but as she meets the person of Christ.

Exclusivity

> *"I'm concerned that my daughter has stopped spending time with her friends. She only wants to be with her boyfriend. She has lost her own opinions and always does what he wants to do. It's like I can't find her anymore."*

This mother came into my (Melissa's) office worried about her fifteen-year-old daughter. She wanted to know what she could do to slow down the intensity of the relationship.

This is a problem we see often in adolescent girls. It has to do with the girl-boy-girl-boy phenomenon. They bounce back and forth from friendships to exclusive dating relationships, and, in these kinds of dating relationships, it is almost as if they have tunnel vision.

In many ways, this is a rite of passage for girls. It is as if they have their chance to fulfill the fairy-tale fable themselves, and so they invest multitudes of time and emotional energy into the relationship. They firmly believe this boy could be the answer to both their longings and their loneliness.

What happens, after a little time, however, is they begin to see that the prince's crown has a few cracks. He chooses to play basketball with his friends rather than take her out. He forgets an event ... or he simply loses his winsome charm. She may even find another boy. Regardless of how the exclusivity dissolves, it is a normal part of a girl's dating life.

As a parent, this is where that back-door philosophy becomes important. For you to tell her that you think the relationship is unhealthy and should end will often make her want to be with him more. What you can do, however, is limit her time with him to one night per weekend. You can allow her only a certain amount of time on the phone or on the Internet. In this way you are slowing down the breakneck speed of their relationship.

You are also slowing down the occasions for them to be involved physically, which all too often accompanies exclusivity.

Promiscuity

Susan had been sexually abused at the age of twelve by her father. By the time she came into my (Sissy's) office, she had averaged ten to twelve boyfriends per year since then.

"I hate my life. No one knows what I'm really like. Everyone at school thinks I'm a slut. My mom does too. I got so tired of hearing it that I decided I might as well give in. I decided to just be one. At least the guys will be nice to me."

Susan has gotten stuck in the boy category of the girl-boy-girl-boy. It is where she feels safe. She has been rejected and hurt by the girls in her grade. Boys compliment her and make her feel good about herself. For Susan, that is more valuable than what she has to give in return.

Sadly, there are many girls just like Susan. Through whatever circumstances have led them there, they have decided that boys are safe and girls are not. So they do whatever they can to connect with those boys.

Susan hung around Daystar for almost a year. In that year, she dealt with the abuse of her father and her poor self-image. She started to believe that she had more to offer than just her body, and she started to make better decisions with guys.

If your daughter is heading down the same road as Susan, help her see that she is more than her physical appearance. Encourage her. Tell her about the strength and the beauty you see inside her—rather than just on the outside. If she is drawn to relationships with guys and uncomfortable around girls, put her in safe groups where she has to build relationships with other girls.

Preventatively, these suggestions can help, as well. Start early in drawing out the deeper beauty in your daughter. Help her find other voices to do this, as well—and not just the voices of her boyfriends. Educate her about sex. Teach her that it is something to look forward to in a marriage relationship. Help her understand *why* God desires purity rather than just the fact that he does (see chapter 6).

Relationships are full of rewards and risks ... regardless of the gender involved. As a parent, there are things you can do that help maximize the rewards and minimize the risks. Here are just a few of our suggestions.

WHAT DOESN'T HELP WHEN SHE IS STRUGGLING

PARENT'S ACTION	GIRL'S REACTION
Minimizing the problem	She shuts down and stops talking to you.
Getting angrier with the friend/boyfriend than she is	She stops seeing her own hurt and feels the need to defend her friend or boyfriend.
Forbidding her from being with certain friends or boys	This creates more intrigue in those friends or boys. (This is unless the situation is dangerous, when she has to be separated for her own physical or emotional safety. Otherwise, try the separation from a back-door strategy.)
Stepping in and fixing the problem for her	She doesn't take responsibility for the situation and doesn't develop her own voice in it.

PARENT'S ACTION	GIRL'S REACTION
Talking negatively or gossiping about her friends	Turns her against you, rather than them.

WHAT HELPS WHEN SHE IS STRUGGLING

PARENT'S ACTION	GIRL'S RESPONSE
Listening	Frees her to be more open
Not giving her answers	Helps her think through solutions herself
Telling her the good that you see in her	Encourages her in spite of the "Oh ... Mom's"
Helping her find places she can connect with other kids	Gives her a safe group of kids who can know, encourage, and challenge her
Having other adults in her life who are encouraging her	Gives her other voices to support what you are wanting her to learn
Talking to her about who she could be friends with	Helps her see that there are girls who may not be in the popular group, but still might make great friends
Helping her look at her role in a situation	Helps her not see herself as the victim, but see that she contributes to the situation
Telling her stories about when you struggled in relationships	Helps her see that she is not alone
Asking her what she thinks would help the situation	Helps her develop problem-solving skills
Helping her understand what she wants is healthy and a part of how God designed her	Keeps her from feeling like something is wrong with her

PARENT'S ACTION	GIRL'S REACTION
Showing her that your relationships are important to you—by the time and energy you invest in them	Helps her feel that it is a good thing to be invested in relationships, and helps her learn what it means to care
Helping her understand what it means to live in a fallen world—relationally, emotionally, and spiritually	She will know not to expect perfection in her relationships or demand that someone meet every need. She will learn that only God can do that.

CHAPTER 9

The Winds of Change

Adolescent girls are like saplings in a hurricane. They are young and vulnerable trees that the winds blow with gale strength.

MARY PIPHER, *REVIVING OPHELIA*

If any of our grandmothers were to overhear a conversation among adolescent girls today, they would think the girls were speaking an entirely new language. They would hear words like *Facebook ... cutting ... texting ... meth.* These words—and these issues—are the newest and some of the most powerful winds of change blowing toward girls.

In this chapter, we would like to address the most potent issues we see facing girls today. Some of these issues will be unfamiliar, and some you may have heard of before. Some will be alarming, and some may be simply the newest way for girls to connect.

As Solomon said, there is nothing new under the sun. Our grandmothers might have had to lean a little closer to find out the meaning behind this new, unintelligible language of girls. But if they did, they would discover that the needs and insecurities behind these winds have been around for countless generations.

MEDIA

It is difficult to even imagine life today without media—magazines, television, movies, music. It infiltrates our lives and our homes—with iPods, HDTVs, TiVo, the Internet. It has its own unintelligible language—and that language speaks strongly into the lives of girls today.

What They're Doing

In May 2005 *Glamour* magazine carried an article entitled "How to Be an It Girl." In that article one section talked about such secrets of the rich and famous as the following:

- Declare yourself gorgeous
- Look like you're having a good time
- RSVP "yes"
- Make your name bigger than you are

These secrets—and the whole idea of being an *it girl*—have nothing to do with who your daughter is. It is all about appearances—physical and social. No authenticity or integrity is developed by a girl who follows these ideas. She is merely becoming more of an image and less of a girl.

This is what media often supports. It's all about looking beautiful, bold, and like you're having a great time. It's about gossiping with friends and getting boys, and it plays directly to the insecurities and the fantasy world of girls.

What's Behind It

Every girl wants to be valued, to be popular. She may feel, at some point during her teenage years, that she really needs a boyfriend to help her achieve these goals. The media preys on these hopes and dreams of teenage girls.

Your daughter's most basic thought pattern is that she is valued for how she acts and what she looks like rather than for who she is. If she were parented by the media, this is where she would remain. She would be a girl who values looking good above all else. She would flaunt her sexuality as a way to get the attention of boys, and she would go to any lengths to keep that attention. She would be bold toward guys and ruthless toward girls.

But fortunately for her, she is not parented by her HDTV or her iPod. She is parented by you—and you have the opportunity to counter this media attack on her values.

What You Can Do

Anne is a friend of ours who has kept much of the media out of her home. Her children play outside, ride bikes, jump on the trampoline, and have their own vegetable garden.

A few years ago, her youngest daughter, Whitney, invited a particular friend to spend the night for the first time. When her friend left the next morning, Whitney described their time together to Anne: "Well, Mom, it was okay. She was nice. But she wanted to do stuff that I thought was boring like watch TV or play on the computer. I couldn't even get her to go outside. I guess she's just not old-fashioned like us."

We love that Anne and her husband have created an old-fashioned home. They read out loud with their children during dinner. They watch movies starring Doris Day and Shirley Temple.

Today, however, the children are all teenagers. They have several computers in their home, and now gather as a family to watch *American Idol*. If it were up to Anne, she would still have things the old-fashioned way, but she is slowly exposing them to the world of media. She started with a foundation built on imagination and creativity and is allowing the media to settle on top of that foundation—rather than being the foundation itself.

We wish every girl could have this type of introduction to the media. Media is a necessary evil in the lives of girls—or at least one that will reach them sooner or later. We believe in the *later*. We think that girls should be exposed to creative and imaginative influences—that they should play outside in the dirt, that they should stretch their legs underneath the sunshine—so that they can come to a fuller understanding of who girls are and what they can be like.

Then comes the *later.* Girls don't need to be sheltered forever —or else the shelter will fall all too loudly as they move away from home. You want to introduce your daughter to the media bit by bit, so that she is able to formulate her own opinions and thoughts while she is under your roof. You want her to learn the concept of discernment, and while she is still at home you have the opportunity to teach it to her. Talk to her about how certain movies or music can affect her spiritually, but ask her opinion first. She will stop listening if she feels you are "preaching." Have a true discussion with her—about the positive and negative sides of whatever she wants to listen to or watch.

Thankfully, Christian publishers and record companies are doing a great job of staying relevant. Many Christian artists and bands are singing positive messages in ways that budding teenage girls will still believe are "cool." Bibles are continually being repackaged in ways that are catching to the critical eyes of adolescents. Christian publishers are also staying ahead of the game with books, fiction and nonfiction, that speak directly to the needs and interests of girls of all ages.

By monitoring the influence of media in your home, you have the opportunity to build the foundation for who your daughter is, rather than whoever the loudest, most scantily clad rock singer of the day is. You can offer her a picture where girls have brains and beauty, where they are strong and feminine, and where who they are is more important than the image they portray.

COMMUNICATION

What They're Doing

Cell phones have taken the world by storm … actually, they have taken the world of teenage girls by storm. Whereas eleven- and twelve-year-olds used to have ponies and bicycles at the tops of their Christmas lists, they now have cell phones. And these are not just ordinary cell phones. These cell phones are like something from a James Bond movie from the 1960s. They allow the user to make phone calls but also allow her to text message (without having to type the entire words—the phone does it for her), take pictures to send to friends, send emails, and even listen to music downloaded from the Internet.

We recently spoke with one teenage girl about her cell phone. "No one calls each other anymore. Why would we? We all text message ... to ask simple questions and even to have longer conversations. It's easy, it's convenient, you don't really have to talk about all of the superficial conversation stuff. And the great thing is you can even do it during class. The teachers don't really catch on."

These girls are in constant communication ... not just through their cell phones but also on the Internet. When email first became a user-friendly option for interaction, you had to dial-up to get connected. Much like writing a letter, you had to compose your message and then send it. Today things are instant. We have become so modernized that even instant messaging is becoming a thing of the past ... it's not instant, or at least not instantly widespread enough.

MySpace, Facebook, and blogs (online journals) clutter the Internet today. Girls have their pictures, their thoughts, and even their journal entries out there for all the world to see. What this means is that each girl, through some type of service like MySpace, posts all her information on her own webpage. That webpage has her picture, her relationship status, things she likes to do, and other information she feels is pertinent. Then, on her "wall" on the page, any people who are her "friends" (meaning they have contacted her and asked if they can be her friend) can post messages to her—with their picture attached.

A concerned mother recently brought me (Sissy) a copy of her fifteen-year-old daughter's MySpace page. It had information on the orgasms of all types of animals ... with various colorful responses from the reader. This young woman is committed to her faith and is what other kids would consider a "good" girl. Her mother was appalled. When confronted by her mother, she said that someone else had put it on her MySpace—and, "It's no big deal anyway. No teenager would think it was anything bad."

Her mother and I both thought it was vulgar and tried to explain to her what others would think if they read the information on her page. She simply didn't understand. This young woman is a product of the technological advances of communication. She was unmoved by what made her mother blush.

This story is but one example of the war that technology is waging on the femininity of our girls. Girls contact boys just as freely as they contact other girls—via cell phones and the Internet. Because of the safety of non–face-to-face interaction, they are bolder and freer. They talk about sex and even mutually carry out sexual acts such as masturbation while they are communicating over the Internet.

Social decorum is also lost on girls who no longer have to go through the casual, "Hi. How are you?" that begins most phone calls. Their communication is abrupt and to the point—without even making full sentences. Girls are losing their charm and the feminine mystique—in one fell swoop.

And this is what girls themselves are doing in terms of communication. We haven't even begun the topic of Internet predators. Thankfully, the creators of sites such as the Facebook are doing their best to prevent predators from having access to girls. Still, the ease with which Internet predators can communicate rises exponentially with the ease with which girls communicate.

What's Behind It

Much of what is behind this communication chaos is simply a girl's longing to connect. When her focus is relationships and, as she reaches adolescence, particularly peer relationships, she has reached nirvana to be able to talk to several of her friends at once—and girls love the fact that they can still communicate during class. Text messaging is just a much more advanced and less noticeable version of note writing.

We have also noticed that girls use this blog concept to reach new heights of attention seeking. If, for example, Susie had her feelings hurt by Allison at school today, she might write about it in her blog that afternoon. She would talk about how her day was her worst in a long time. Whether she mentions Allison by name or not, Susie may use that blog as a way of getting back at Allison. Teenage girls can and sometimes will use any method possible to get the attention or revenge they feel they are due.

What You Can Do

Computer and cell phones are both a blessing and a curse in the world of girls. The advantage of cell phones is that parents can get in touch with girls immediately when they need to. They help facilitate pickups from practice and safety in cars.

Computer courses are part of the curriculum of many schools today. Kids start using computers as early as kindergarten and are given computers by the schools (actually their parents pay a hefty sum for them) as young as middle school. Grades and homework are posted via the Internet. It is impossible, in today's time, to keep computers out of homes.

What you can do, however, is slow down the pace of your daughter's use of technology. Girls don't need cell phones until they are spending significant amounts of time away from you—whether in activities or driving a car. Even then, cell phone use can be heavily restricted. You can make sure she doesn't use her phone after a specific time at night. You can give her a certain amount of minutes per month, and thankfully, you can receive billing statements that give you a full report of her calls and text messages.

With computers, you can use the same theory. Girls don't even need access to computers until they are school age. Providing crayons and paper rather than computers does wonders for the creativity level of very young brains. Once she does have access to computers, your daughter always needs to know that you are her computer guardian. This guardianship is easier when the computer is in a common room, rather than in hers. Walk through the room regularly and look over her shoulder. If she clicks out of something quickly, you know you may need to do a little more sleuthing.

There are fantastic programs today to monitor and block certain websites on the Internet. We also tell parents to tell their daughters that whatever is posted in cyberspace is free game for parents, as well. We have parents who set up MySpace accounts just to monitor their daughter's activities. This is not only to check on her, but also to check for potential predators.

Girls need lots of instruction and guidance as to computer safety. Because they are naive and developmentally fearless, they are not aware of the dangers inherent in the Internet. They need your help—and your monitoring. Again, this monitoring should taper off as she moves closer to eighteen. She needs to be making her own choices, because she will do so unhindered when she leaves home. But especially as she begins her Internet experience and throughout middle and early high school, she needs your help, and that help also teaches her the value of discernment.

Fortunately, cell phones and Internet have other benefits. Both are great leverage. If your daughter is acting trustworthy, give her a little more rope on these freedoms. If she messes up, pull that rope right back in. Because relationships are so important, these two methods of communication pack a lot of power.

SCHOOL CULTURE

I (Melissa) recently spoke with a group of seventh- and eighth-grade girls about their purpose in life. They each talked about where they saw themselves fifteen years from now. One girl in the group talked about how much she looked forward to being a mom. Another girl turned to her and said, "Wow. That's really great. You just don't hear that very often anymore."

I was shocked. When we (Melissa and Sissy) were growing up, being a mom is what most girls wanted. These changes are not just the result of the women's movement. They are also a result of the culture in schools today.

What They're Doing

Expectations for girls have been raised considerably in the past twenty years. Girls know that they are just as able to be a doctor as they are a nurse, or a college professor as they are a school teacher—and they are also able to be stay-at-home moms. Their career options know no bounds. This is a tremendous advancement in terms of gender roles.

Girls have risen to meet these expectations. Fifty-seven percent of college students in 2005 were girls. But many of these girls are overstressed. Why? What is causing the pressure these girls feel? Is it societal expectations, academic pressures, or the internal world of girls?

What's Behind It

Without a doubt, academic pressure has risen in recent years. We have parents of fifth graders tell us their daughters spend four hours doing homework per night. Schools are much more forward thinking in terms of college preparation, all of which increases the workload that boys and girls experience—especially in middle and high school.

Girls are also involved in a flurry of activities. They are on soccer teams, run cross-country, play lacrosse, take art lessons, piano lessons, write for the school newspaper, and try to maintain the all-important social life. The combination of these activities does make one's head spin.

But this combination is not what we would say is the primary cause of a girl's stress. I (Sissy) met with a high school senior named Danielle who was experiencing pretty high levels of anxiety. When I asked her what had been the most recent cause, she told me this story. "Everyone in the drama department at my school had to participate in the school play. We had to be there for about four hours every day. I also had been chosen to run in the state track meet—which was a huge honor. I didn't know what to do. My track coach was calling the drama teacher, and they were arguing about where I should be. I knew both teachers would be disappointed, and I got really upset."

Activities consumed this young girl's time and took over her schedule, but what consumed her heart was the fear of disappointing someone. As we have continually said, it all goes back to relationships.

More is expected from girls today. There are more opportunities than ever before ... and more activities in which to participate. This definitely makes for busy girls, and at some point, girls' schedules may need to be pared down. But where girls hit the real stress is in their need to please.

What You Can Do

As Danielle and I talked, we talked about the idea of finding her own voice (see chapter 5). We often teach girls to be nice, sometimes at the expense of their own peace of mind. There is a difference between being committed to kindness and being committed to pleasing others. Girls often don't know how to distinguish between the two.

This is where we can help. We can help girls learn to be aware of the feelings of another, without having to take responsibility for those feelings. Danielle is working on making her own decisions and being okay with disappointing others.

Usually the disappointment of others has more to do with the one who is disappointed than with the one who does the disappointing. To help girls learn to act in ways that are kind and consistent with who they are and what God would want is to bring freedom to these girls whose goal is simply to please.

It is also helpful for girls to know that they don't have to be the best in every activity in which they participate. Because they have so many opportunities, and because it's their nature to want to please others, girls often believe they have to excel in every opportunity. It does a girl's heart good to know that you will love her just as much on the B team as the A team. A's are great on report cards, but not a prerequisite to her being valued. Help her see that who she is is not based on her performance—in any area. Encourage her when she succeeds and when she fails. Tell her you are proud of her when she makes a goal in soccer and when she misses the ball. Regardless of how she acts toward you, your daughter does want to please you, and because of that, you have a great deal to offer her in terms of what should dictate her value as a person.

Exercise also makes a tremendous difference in the stress level of girls. It touches on a variety of her needs at once. It keeps her in good health and can help her feel better about her body when it's in shape. Also, to have a physical outlet for stress, anxiety, and anger can help clear her mind. She is then able to focus with a little less pressure and a few more natural endorphins.

DRUGS AND ALCOHOL

What They're Doing

Drugs and alcohol have been issues for teenagers for generations. What has changed, however, are the drugs of choice. According to the National Institute on Drug Abuse, illicit drug use has declined significantly since its peak years in 1996 and 1997. Alcohol use among teenagers since that time has also decreased, although it is still the most widely used drug among young people. Marijuana use has basically remained stable, as well as tobacco use.

What has increased is the use of prescription drugs and inhalants. These are actually two types of drug use we hear about frequently in our offices. We see kids who abuse alcohol, marijuana, and even heavier drugs such as cocaine and ecstasy. But there are also those that are a little more accessible—like in the pantry or medicine cabinet. Ritalin, Vicodin, and OxyContin are being used more prevalently among teenagers today. They even trade these drugs at "pharming" parties. These drugs are easy to get, as many teenagers take Ritalin on a daily basis or are given prescriptions for painkillers after various procedures. They are as near as the closest medicine cabinet. Teenagers also consider these drugs safer, without knowing they can cause addictions and serious side effects.

Teenagers will use over-the-counter medicines, as well. We have talked to girls who have used cough syrups and cold medicines, anything that will take them away from their problems.

The inhalants teenagers use vary from household items such as spray paint and hairspray to correction fluid and felt-tip markers. They sniff these directly from their containers, pour them onto fabric to sniff from, or spray them into bags.

Basically, if your teenage daughter is determined to get a buzz, she will use just about anything she can get her hands on, from liquor in your cabinet to cocaine she can get at school to medicines in her bathroom at home.

What's Behind It

Basically, what is behind a teenager's desire to do drugs are two things. First, teenagers have a deep need to take risks. They want to live life on the edge. This edge can be positive activities such as rock climbing, serving as student council president, or being a camp counselor, or destructive activities such as driving too fast or drug and alcohol use.

Regardless of the activity, this risk-taking activity builds their self-images. They feel good about themselves as they accomplish something difficult. It helps them feel a sense of significance and adventure. That adventure can be drinking six beers in one night or smoking pot before they go to soccer practice—or it can be some of the more positive activities we have mentioned.

The second reason behind the desire to take drugs is the deep angst that many teenagers live with. Girls grapple with relationship issues: struggles with girlfriends and insecurities with boyfriends. They may be going through family and academic stresses as well. Many girls today live in a state of tension—with a great deal of pressure and pain compounded with the normal adolescent issues.

Drugs and alcohol provide an easy escape. Temporarily, at least, they transport these girls to a place with no pressure, giving them a sense of freedom from stress and pain they rarely feel in their daily lives.

What You Can Do

For starters, you can talk to your girls about drugs and alcohol. The Partnership for a Drug-Free America says that teenagers whose parents talk to them about the risks of drugs are 42 percent less likely to use drugs than those who don't. Still, only one in four adolescents report having these conversations.

You can also have other voices in their lives, as we talked

about in chapters 7 and 8—voices of adults and teens whom you trust and are not participating in these types of destructive activities. As an incentive, we only allow those kids who are not using drugs or alcohol to act as counselors for our younger kids' summer camps. Try to find built-in rewards for your daughter when she is not using.

Finally, we believe a strong spiritual life is the best prevention against the abuse of drugs and alcohol. If you are involved in a church that you love but doesn't have a vibrant youth group, you may want to allow her to go to a different youth group or attend a parachurch organization. She needs support—as she will be surrounded by kids who may not be a positive encouragement to your daughter.

If you suspect your daughter might be experimenting with drugs and/or alcohol, stay up until she comes home or make sure she wakes you up. Have her kiss you good-night so you can look into her eyes and smell her breath. Watch for secretive behaviors or a sudden change in friends. If you find something in her room, it is probably not her friend's, even though she may tell you the opposite. Be a good detective, but don't accuse her until you know the facts.

And if you catch her having used drugs or alcohol, give her consequences! We see parents often who simply tell their daughters how they experimented themselves when they were her age. This just helps girls know that they can play around with drugs and alcohol and then turn out fine—just like their parents.

If you suspect that she might have a problem, get help—especially if the use is frequent or involves heavier drugs like cocaine, crystal meth, or ecstasy. Regardless of her basketball or cheerleading schedule, please intervene before it's too late. Addictions only get worse with time, and the risk-taking types of behavior increase. She needs your help to stop and to stop immediately if there is a problem.

CUTTING/SELF-MUTILATION

What They're Doing

"I would rather see myself bleed than feel myself hurt."

These are the kinds of comments we hear from girls who engage in what is referred to as *self-mutilation*. Eight years ago, I (Sissy) met with one girl who cut herself on her arm. She was struggling with depression, and I had her parents drive her straight to the psychiatric hospital.

Today, three to four out of every ten teenage girls I see in my counseling office have experimented with self-mutilation, or, as it is more commonly known, "cutting." The *Journal of Abnormal Psychology* reported that 14 to 39 percent of adolescents participate in some kind of self-harming behavior.

Girls hurt themselves in all locations and with all manner of objects. They scratch their arms with paper clips. They cut their legs with scissors or cut their stomachs or breasts with knives. Typically, the cuts are surface wounds. They are deep enough to draw blood, but not to sever a major artery, and, most importantly to these girls, they are deep enough to make them think about external, rather than internal pain.

What's Behind It

As adults, it's hard to understand what could ever be behind self-mutilation. It is appalling to think about your daughter hurting herself for any reason, but girls do—and for a host of reasons that make complete sense to them.

From a physical standpoint, the brains of these girls respond to the injury in a way that encourages the behavior. Opiates are released from the brain when a body is injured—to dull the pain. These opiates that dull the physical pain of the cut serve to dull the emotional pain, as well.

Emotionally, cutting finds its origins in many of the same issues as eating disorders. Control and self-hatred fuel the marks these girls make on their bodies. Their world feels out of control emotionally. It may be social, academic, or family stressors. Whatever the reason, cutting is a way to control their own pain ... rather than just have it inflicted upon them.

Self-hatred, as we have mentioned, is a powerful force in the world of adolescent girls. As they cut, they get back at the person they often feel is the most flawed—themselves. They can take out their anger in this way, even though the anger often should be directed at someone else. Again, it is in her control to direct it at herself. She finds resolution to the pain.

Indeed, that is possibly the most significant reason girls cut: it works. It does bring resolution. This reason compounds the problem. Because it works, girls do it again—and again, until they are left with scars on the outside which point to scars that are much deeper.

The other danger of cutting is that it has gotten lots of hype in the past few years—hype that is not necessarily negative from an adolescent girl's perspective. Girls are talking about it at school. They are going to chat rooms on the Internet to talk to other cutters. Celebrities are "coming out" about their own self-mutilation.

Because it is edgy enough to appeal to the rebelliousness of teenagers and because, from their perspective, it accomplishes its purported goal, the word spreads. At Daystar, we have to be very careful about allowing girls to talk in our groups about cutting. They can easily get ideas from each other.

Tragically, cutting has become a fad in the world of girls today. But as girls learn safer, more productive outlets for their pain and stress, they tell us that cutting loses its luster. A fifteen-year-old recently told us she had cut for the first time in a year because her boyfriend had broken up with her, and much to our delight, she told us, "It just didn't work for me anymore."

What You Can Do About It

If cutting is emotionally and socially motivated, it can be difficult, as a parent, to know how to respond. As counselors, we have the same rule of thumb about cutting that we do with kids who threaten suicide.

We tell parents that if their child threatens to take her life, put her in the car and drive her to the emergency room. If she means it, she needs to be taken, and the ER will do a psychiatric evaluation to determine what needs to happen next. If she is manipulating you, she needs to know that you take that kind of threat seriously—that threatening suicide is not a way to express her anger that you won't let her stay out an hour later with her boyfriend. If the reason is manipulative, she will see that this kind of tactic is not going to work—before you ever reach the hospital. If she is serious, you have her in the care of professionals.

With cutting, the same holds true. If your daughter is in enough pain to take it out on her body, she needs to talk with a counselor or get a psychiatric evaluation. If she is motivated by more attention-seeking means, she may also need a counselor's help to discover more positive ways to find acceptance. And again, she needs to know that you take any kind of self-destructive action seriously.

In either situation, your daughter needs to talk. She may be embarrassed and hesitant to talk to you in the beginning, but she needs an outlet other than one involving self-mutilation.

First, she needs to learn to express verbally what is going on internally. It helps tremendously to put words to what she is feeling. As she comes to understand the reasons she is cutting, she can find more positive coping strategies. Art, exercise, and writing are three avenues we believe help girls release emotional pain—without injuring their bodies. They produce rather than destroy.

If you suspect your daughter may be cutting, it is completely appropriate to ask her to show you her arms. Watch for thick bracelets or long sleeves when the weather is hot. If she comes home from school in despair, disappears for thirty minutes, and reemerges happy, she could be self-mutilating.

Cutting is a complicated, frightening fad for girls today. It is also one that is cloaked in darkness from a spiritual standpoint. It is done in secrecy and lulls the cutter into believing it truly does help.

But we have seen girls who begin to understand the destructiveness—physically, emotionally, and spiritually. As they talk about their pain, as they find other ways to release it, and as they look to God for guidance and support, these girls experience his healing.

EATING DISORDERS

> *"I realized today that I've been wasting a lot of my life trying to achieve this goal of being thin. I've spent so much time and energy focusing on it and it now controls my life. It controls all my thoughts. I'm stuck and I can't get out. Every time I think I'm doing good and I have the strength to get through, I fall back down again. I'm sick and tired of living this way. I wish I could just accept the way I am and not freak out so much about my weight. I have so much regret for how I've been living my life. I'm giving myself over to this god of thinness."*

What They're Doing

This fifteen-year-old girl is not alone in giving herself over to the god of thinness. According to the Anorexia Nervosa and Related Eating Disorders, Inc. (ANRED), eating disorders affect almost 5 percent of young women in the United States. *Anorexia* is defined as an eating disorder marked by an extreme fear of becoming overweight leading to excessive dieting to the point of serious ill-health and sometimes death. It affects 1 percent of female adolescents. Bulimia, a condition in which bouts of overeating are followed by undereating, use of laxatives, or self-induced vomiting, affects 1 to 3 percent of middle and high school girls.

The same study reported that 15 percent of young women have unhealthy attitudes and behaviors about food. These attitudes and behaviors are not new. For generations, women have been struggling with the way they look.

I (Melissa) remember staying in the gym longer than the other kids so that they would have already changed and left by the time I got to the locker room. I (Sissy) remember dieting in high school to try to keep up with my beautiful, petite friends.

But in the sixties and the eighties, when each of us were teenagers, neither of us remembers hearing of girls who struggled with eating disorders. (They were surely there but often in secret and certainly not with the same frequency.) We remember wanting to be attractive and feeling uncomfortable in our skin—or our body. But we don't remember the pressure to have no body fat and the obsession with "healthy" eating.

Today, every girl we counsel has a friend or knows someone with an eating disorder. They hear of girls in counseling and going to treatment centers regularly. Girls watch each other's food intake and follow each other to the bathroom at school to make sure their friends are not throwing up.

I (Melissa) counseled a girl recently who, as a size six, said she hated her body. She told me that she guessed a zero would be a size that would be acceptable, although she really wanted to be thinner. The role models for girls today are either computer generated or have eating disorders themselves. A desirable body is not just slim—it is almost nonexistent.

What's Behind It

Several years ago I (Melissa) told a group of parents that eating disorders were often a "good girl's" way to rebel. The generalizations typically do fit for girls with eating disorders. Most are bright, active, and perfectionistic. They push themselves to make grades that are outstanding, have relationships that are always positive, and perform flawlessly in every activity in which they participate.

Eating disorders can be particularly trapping for Christian girls who have a more perfectionistic bent. Not only do they feel the pressure from themselves to perform well, they also can get into a legalistic way of thinking in which God is more concerned with their outward behavior than the state of their heart. They have to make good grades, excel in all activities, and live 100 percent of the time in ways that are honoring to God.

To put it simply, grace and eating-disordered thinking are often completely at odds with each other. But once again, eating disorders serve a purpose. It is easier to focus on food than on the pain inside. It is easier to be angry with yourself for purging than for hurting someone you care for.

These girls exert a lot of control—often on themselves and in the amount of food they eat, since they can't control their environment. When I (Sissy) first began counseling in 1993, approximately seven out of every ten girls I saw with eating disorders had been sexually abused. This correlation exists for several reasons.

First, these girls had something happen to them that was entirely out of their control (although most of them felt tremendous shame for not controlling it). Therefore, they lived their lives trying to recapture that control. Food intake—or the lack of it—was something that no one else could dictate, so it became the focus of their need to control.

Because of the abuse, their sexuality also became a source of profound shame. To gain weight would cover up their sexuality, so that no one would see them as a sexual being. To lose weight would help that sexuality to disappear, and return them to a prepubescent body.

Today, maybe one or two out of every ten girls we see with eating disorders has been sexually abused. The lack of control has other origins—familial, social, academic, athletic. One girl may not play as well as she thinks she should in soccer. Another may feel that she lets her parents down with her schoolwork. Another may believe that no one at school likes her. Several girls I (Sissy) counsel have simply been told, either by friends or parents, that they were overweight.

Girls struggle with body image. Whether they experience minor discomfort or hatred of their bodies, all girls will grapple with this issue at some time or another. But when girls feel out of control and put a lot of pressure on themselves to perform, they are often set up for an eating disorder.

Performance is a huge issue for girls struggling with anorexia and bulimia, but what happens is that body image unconsciously becomes a catch-all for these girls. If she feels that her friends are disappointed in her, she gets angry with herself for being overweight. If she doesn't make the A she thought she should have on a history test, she makes herself throw up. Basically, whatever she does not like about herself all flows through the funnel of her body.

Therefore, to punish her body brings relief. She hates herself, so she throws up. It is almost as if she is purging herself of all that is "wrong" with her. She is angry with herself, so she doesn't allow herself to eat often without knowing why. These activities answer both her need for control and her need to express her anger toward herself.

What You Can Do About It

Girls with eating disorders characteristically are unable to express themselves. They can't talk about what they feel, because they usually don't know how they feel. I (Melissa) met with a fifteen-year-old with anorexia whom I asked to keep a daily journal of her feelings. She came back to me a week later with a list of what she had eaten each day and how she felt about it. All her feelings had to do with food and her body. Why? It was safe for her. It was easier for her to feel disgust for her body than disappointment over her relationships.

The first step we would take with a girl struggling with an eating disorder would be to help her reconnect to her feelings. We would help her learn to talk about her sadness, anger, grief, shame, and all the other emotions that flood our hearts each day. We would help her reconnect to her longings for relationship, because those longings have been numbed by her preoccupation with food.

We would also help her see that her value goes beyond the boundaries of her physical being. Girls with eating disorders need to see that they have things to offer besides their physical appearance and their perfect performance. They can be good friends ... they can volunteer with younger children ... they can be artists who don't have to color inside the lines.

Most importantly, any girl struggling with an eating disorder needs to be overwhelmed by grace. She needs your grace as a parent when she causes her soccer team to lose or makes her first C on a report card. Consequences still apply, at times, but she needs to know that your love for her is not related to her performance.

Ultimately, she needs to know the grace of a loving God. She needs to see that God's love reaches down into her weakest and most insecure places. He loves her as she is and not as she believes she should be.

As a parent, this probably feels overwhelming. Eating disorders are that way . . . for her and for you. They are highly addictive and become all-consuming for your daughter. If you suspect that she might be struggling with an eating disorder, seek professional help. Take her to someone who can help her work through the deep issues involved, not someone who will just give her a list of "healthy" and "unhealthy" behaviors and give her advice about food. That just creates more anxiety. As we have said before, make sure that person is one that you trust spiritually—one who will help be an instrument of God's grace,

Find her a good nutritionist too. You don't need to be her food police. She will only fight you harder for that control. We recommend a nutritionist to help with the food and a counselor to help with the emotional and spiritual components of eating disorders. You can't do this alone. You need other adults who can be on her team, encouraging and challenging her to be the wonderfully imperfect girl God has created her to be.

Eating disorders are a terrible battle to fight for any girl. They are complicated addictions because, unlike alcohol or drugs, she will have food as a part of every day of her life. Eating disorders are also frightening for a parent, as you often watch her disappear before your eyes.

In all of these areas, you and your daughter need support. You need other voices to help and to walk alongside you both in this process of your daughter becoming who she is meant to be. With the effects of media, technology, school culture, drugs and alcohol, cutting, eating disorders—girls today are under attack from within themselves and from the world around them. As Mary Pipher said, "They are young and vulnerable trees." And these are strong winds blowing against them.

PART THREE

How Can I Help?

CHAPTER 10

Seeing Clearly

> ***We determine by our inner dialogue and predispositions—fears, angers, and judgments—much more than we'd like to admit. We determine what we will see and what we won't see, what we pay attention to and what we don't. That's why we have to clean the lens: we have to get our ego-agenda out of the way, so we can see things as they are.***
>
> RICHARD ROHR, *EVERYTHING BELONGS*

Although Father Richard Rohr was talking about prayer, he could have just as well been speaking of parenting. In many ways, parenting is the least egocentric job in the world. Your time—at least a good majority of it—is spent doing things for your daughter, listening to her, talking with her, and thinking about her.

But our own ego-agendas always seem to creep in to cloud our vision: our fears, angers, judgments, and various other unresolved issues. A mother who struggles with her weight is harder on her overweight daughter than on her thin daughter. A father who excelled in sports pushes his daughter to run cross-country, when all she really wants to do is dance.

Ego-agendas are rarely on purpose. You would not purposely rely on your daughter to take the emotional place of your ex-wife. You would not fulfill your own unmet adolescent needs through her. But parents often do. Counselors do, as well.

Countertransference is a word that bounces around every graduate school for therapists. It is defined as "a process that sometimes occurs in therapy where repressed emotions in the therapist are awakened by identification with the experiences and feelings of the patient." What this means is that the girls that I (either one of us, actually) have the most difficulty counseling are the ones who bring up my own issues, who remind me of parts of myself that I don't like, or who have opportunities that I could only long for in my past. They awaken my feelings, whether I know it or not.

As it applies to parents, *countertransference* could thus be defined as "a process that happens often in parenting where repressed emotions in the parent are awakened by identification with the experiences and feelings of the child."

In graduate school we weren't told what to do *if* countertransference happened, but *when* countertransference happened. Parents, teachers, counselors—anyone who cares for girls—will have emotional awakenings. The lens then becomes cloudy, and our ability to see the girl we love becomes blurred.

HOW TO TELL WHERE YOUR LENS IS CLOUDY

- Would you rather be with your child when you are upset than with your spouse or close friends?
- Do you feel more disappointed than your child when she is not chosen for certain teams or activities?
- Do you put pressure on her to do the things you did or to take advantages of opportunities you were not given?
- Is it important to you that your daughter see you as "cool"?
- Do you find yourself allowing her to get away with things you got away with as a teenager?
- Do you regularly get angry at one child more than the other?
- Do you hear themes in the way you criticize your child?
- Is your anger or frustration with her sometimes stronger than the situation warrants?

We would imagine you answered yes to at least one of these questions. Because of our fallen states, we all have cloudy lenses. The question is not *if*, therefore, but *where.*

We see parents with cloudy lenses frequently in our offices. It is not that they mean for their lenses to be cloudy; it is that their own needs, insecurities, and fallenness inadvertently color their parenting. What happens, as a result, is that the children seen through these clouded lenses each take on a very specific role in response.

The Comfort Child

Last summer at camp, a junior in high school came to me (Sissy) to ask if she could call her father. When I reminded her of our rule against phone calls, her eyes filled with tears and her voice took on an edge of panic. "But I have to call my dad. He gets really worried about me. I need to tell him I'm okay. You don't understand what he's like. He won't be able to sleep at night if I don't talk to him."

This father, who loves his daughter deeply, is also leaning on her in ways that are detrimental to her. His is a more extreme example, but it also happens in little ways.

Some dear friends of ours tragically lost a baby in their third trimester of pregnancy. They were understandably heartbroken. Their two-year-old daughter noticed their tears and wanted to comfort them. She tried to make them laugh, crawled in their laps, and tried to distract them with her toys. They caught on quickly to what their daughter was doing. They told her that it was not her job to make mommy and daddy feel better. It was their job to comfort her, and it was okay to be sad.

What a powerful lesson for Caroline to have learned at two. Even as a little girl, she is aware. Girls are typically tuned in to the nuances of your behaviors and emotions (maybe with the exception of those in the Narcissistic Years). They will notice your sadness and often try to be a source of comfort—in small ways or in big.

At times this can be okay ... even a good thing. For your daughter to be kind to you when she knows you are having a bad day helps her learn compassion. For her to clean the kitchen when you are stressed teaches her shared responsibility. But these actions are based on her choice rather than your unspoken emotional requirement.

We believe a daughter's need to provide comfort becomes a concern when it follows a pattern. If your daughter believes it is her job to comfort you, she will feel too much power. If she feels that she is the only one who can help you get through a situation or if she believes you need her to be okay, she will feel too much power.

It can also, unconsciously, become a sweet source of support for you. It is easy to enjoy her hugs and kindness—especially if you are lonely. Then gradually a pattern is set. She feels confident in her role as caretaker, and you, often unknowingly, enjoy her care. Thus the lens becomes cloudy.

As we've said before, your daughter needs to feel that you are stronger than she is. It helps her feel safe and cared for. So watch for comforting patterns in her behavior. Notice if she writes you a note or gives you a hug every time you are stressed. Watch to see if she crawls into your bed with you every time you seem sad. Help her know, like our friends did, that it is not her job to comfort you. You are the parent. It is your job to comfort her, and sometimes it is okay to be sad.

The Redemption Child

I (Melissa) recently met with a young soccer player named Andrea. She was to compete in a state tournament but had to choose between the tournament and a family trip to Europe that had been planned for six months. When she told her coach, the coach became angry. This was Andrea's response to the coach's anger: "I hate that my parents are making me go on the trip. Not that I don't want to go, but I just feel bad hurting my coach. She was a really good soccer player when she was in high school and would give anything to get to play in this tournament."

Andrea is acting as a redemption child for her soccer coach. She is fulfilling her coach's dreams and wishes for her life. We also see this happen in families. A parent who loved cheerleading makes her daughter try out for cheerleading year after year, when the daughter hates it and is more creative than athletic. Or a father makes his athletic daughter take art lessons twice a week because his parents discouraged his artistic inclinations while he was growing up.

These parents can't see past their own unfulfilled dreams or glory days. They don't seem to care about the desires or even the talents of their daughter. The parents are either reliving the life they lived or living the life they wanted but never had—through their child. The lens is cloudy.

What often happens is that the kids become angry. They feel that who they are doesn't matter to their parents as much as who their parents want them to be. So they fail on purpose or start to pull away emotionally from their parents.

There are times to make your daughter participate in different activities (see chapter 3). She needs to experience a variety of interests before she is able to discover her passions and her talents. But she will have passions and talents that may well be different than yours. As she grows older, it is important that she discover her own identity apart from yours, and she needs to feel your love and admiration whether she is an artist, an athlete, or just your independent-minded little girl.

The Buddy Child

A friend of ours named Leanne told us she wanted to have a baby because she moved to a new town and needed a buddy. Leanne is a great mom. Her daughter, who is now eight, knows that her mom is her mom and not just her buddy—but some girls don't.

We see parents who would rather be liked by their daughter than respected. These are the parents who tell their teenage daughters of their own wild days in high school. They share their personal lives like they are roommates rather than mothers or fathers and daughters.

We (Sissy and Melissa) have both liked the television show *The Gilmore Girls*, but as we watched the mother-daughter relationship evolve, we often became nervous. The first few seasons showed Lorelai and her teenage daughter, Rory. Lorelai is a character who is fun, wacky, and quick, but she is also more of a roommate to Rory than a mom. During the shows we would both talk to the television, saying things like, "No, Lorelai, don't let your boyfriend sleep over. Rory is in the next room!" But Lorelai did. Rory knew all about her mother's life—to her own detriment. In turn, Rory's response was one that we see happen often. Rory became an adult at a young age. As a teenager, she actually became more responsible than her mother.

The other response we see happen is that girls will join the party. Because a girl knows her mother had sex before marriage, she doesn't feel that purity really matters. Her father smoked a lot of marijuana and is now a really good guy, so she can too, she feels.

These children are comfortable around their parents—too comfortable. Girls need boundaries. You will have the rest of your life to be your daughter's friend—and your friendship will not suffer for having disciplined her as she grew up. Boundaries help her feel safe and grounded.

Girls who get away with the worst they are capable of begin to see themselves that way. They see themselves as bad or selfish or easy. As you give your daughter boundaries and discipline, you help her be the best she can be. You help her know that you believe in who she is and who she can be.

The Extension Child

> *"It was so sad for me to watch my daughter as she left school. The other kids congregated in a group and were hugging each other good-bye. She walked right by them to my car. I think she must feel really isolated and left out."*

As this mother and I (Melissa) talked, I realized that she was interpreting how she would feel in her daughter's situation. She was feeling her own emotional response rather than that of her daughter. Her daughter was fine. She is a twelve-year-old who is just as happy to be with a few, close friends as she is to read in her room alone for hours. She is embarrassed by the overly demonstrative shows of affection of many teenage girls. But her mom would have been right in the middle of it when she was twelve.

We all do this at times. We believe others want what we want, need what we need, and think the way we think—and parents feel protective of their children. So a mother whose daughter has not been invited to a party may be more hurt about the situation than her nine-year-old. A father may be more disappointed that his daughter was not elected student body president than she is. These girls are extensions of their parents. Again, the lens is cloudy.

To some degree, this extension theory is natural. When your daughter is in public and behaves badly, it reflects on you. If she gets into trouble with her friends and other parents find out, they talk about her as the "Jones girl." Your children are extensions of you, but they are extensions who have their own identities and will have to face their own consequences.

We have seen many mothers who unconsciously think of their oldest daughters as extension children. They take for granted their strengths and are hard on their weaknesses. In essence, they treat them in much the same way as they treat themselves.

I (Sissy) meet with a mother who is much harder on her daughter than she is on her son. She is more like her daughter and expects a great deal from her. The mother doesn't want to be coddled, so she doesn't coddle her daughter, but she does take extra care of her son. It is hard for her to say that she is proud of her daughter, but she will freely talk about her son's accomplishments.

Your daughter is made up of your genes—the good and the bad ones. She has parts of your personality, mannerisms, and looks. But she is her own person. For you to be proud of a strength she has that is similar to yours doesn't mean you are bragging about yourself. For you to criticize a weakness in her doesn't change it in you. As you begin to see her as a separate person, she is freer to become that person—with all her own strengths and weaknesses.

HOW TO CLEAN A LENS

Maybe you recognize yourself in one of the patterns. You're starting to see a few smudges on your parenting lens that affect the way you see your daughter. Now what do you do? How do you clean the lens in a way that enables you to see her clearly? We have three practical suggestions:

- Divide your wood
- Allow yourself to be average
- Let go of the perfect picture

Divide Your Wood

How can you say to your brother, "Let me take the speck out of your eye," when all the time there is a plank in your own eye? You hypocrite, first take the plank out of your own eye, and then you will see clearly to remove the speck from your brother's eye.

MATTHEW 7:4–5

This verse is a little more confusing when it comes to parenting. What happens is the plank in your eye stretches all the way over to your daughter's and ends in a little speck in hers. Your plank and her speck is often one and the same—or so it feels. Just as it is hard to sometimes know where you end and she begins, it is hard to know where your plank turns into her speck.

For example, I (Sissy) met with a mother and daughter. The mother is extremely frustrated with her teenage daughter who is failing several classes. She asks her every day about her homework and gets more and more angry when her daughter hasn't done it. Doesn't sound like a plank. Sounds much more like the speck is the problem.

But the mother's mounting anger tells us there is a plank somewhere. Her husband died six months ago. She tells anyone who tries to help that she's fine, but her fist is clenching tighter and tighter around her daughter. Her plank is her unwillingness to grieve. She is trying to control her emotions by controlling her daughter.

As I met with the two of them, I tried to get them to divide the wood. The mother needed to see how her grief was exacerbating her anger and need to control her daughter. The daughter needed to take responsibility for her grades. Planks and specks, specks and planks.

As a parent, life will crowd you as you try to love your daughter. It may be your past life, your present life, or your fear of the future that bring about your planks.

All of a sudden, you hear your own parent's voice in your inner ear as you tell your daughter she needs to lose weight. It will feel impossible to discipline objectively when your husband has just left you. You will be afraid to allow her to do certain things because of your own fears of what could be.

Listen to your life. Try to determine what are your planks and what are her specks. Journal. Talk to friends or to your spouse.

Notice if you are frustrated regularly with your daughter or with one child more than the others. Is it a situation that repeatedly awakens your emotions with her? Are their other issues crowding in on you that could affect your parenting?

These questions will help you sort out your planks from her specks. If you're still having trouble, contact a counselor who could see either you or the two of you together. As you find where your wood separates from hers, you will be able to see her a little more clearly and give yourself a little more grace.

Allow Yourself to Be Average

I (Melissa) went snow skiing recently for the first time since I had a head injury over ten years ago. My accident affected my balance and my response time, so I was nervous. I told Sissy and Mimi I wouldn't even ski with them the first day. I had to concentrate. I wanted to be able to ski just like I used to. I got out there, and I couldn't make my boots feel comfortable. I couldn't figure out how to pick up my ski on the turn. I didn't remember where to plant my pole. The harder I tried, the more tense and frustrated I became—then I just got tired.

I decided to call it a day and go home. My way home took me down an easier slope. All of a sudden, I realized I was enjoying myself. Instead of thinking the people around me were in my way, I started being friendly. I noticed the beauty of the mountains and the trees. I was actually having fun. It was then that I realized it's really okay to be an average skier.

I told this story to a MOPS (Mothers of Preschoolers) group recently. I told them that my skiing experience was a lot like parenting. To try to be a great parent only makes you tense, frustrated, and tired. It is okay to be average. Average parents are freed up to enjoy their children and see them through cleaner lenses.

As I spoke that morning, I really didn't have to teach much about this idea. Their response—actually, their relief—was immediate. Every woman who spoke to me afterward told me how thankful she was to know that it was okay to be average.

There is perhaps more pressure today than there has ever been on parents to do it "right." You hear voices saying, "Spend quality time with each of your children" ... "Teach them about Jesus, but not in a legalistic way" ... "Talk to them about drugs, sex, and alcohol before it's too late" ... "Make sure they have good self-esteem" ... "Get them in the right school at the right time" ... "Give them every opportunity." It's enough to make you a very frustrated skier!

Don't worry so much about where you plant your poles. Like me, you may have to make a conscious decision to let go. Yes, we want you to look at your own life, and yes, there are a lot of practical tips even in this book ... let alone all of the wonderful parenting books you already have stacked beside your bedside table. But you are not going to get it all right. What your daughter wants—what your daughter needs—is not a perfect parent. She needs *you.*

Let Go of the Perfect Picture

Alcoholics Anonymous has a statement that "Expectations are preconceived resentments." They are also foretold disappointments. But they are resentments and disappointments that every person who becomes a parent carries with them into their new family.

I recently met with a family whose daughter had been sent to a wilderness program. Before she left, she was sneaking out every night to meet different boys. She was drinking and using drugs. Basically, she was uncontrollable.

She was now home. She had been home for one month without getting into trouble. Her parents and I were thrilled, but as the conversation came around to how each of her parents were doing, her mother dissolved into tears. "I am so proud of Courtney. I can tell she has really tried. She has put all of this behind her and is doing great. But I'm not. I can't seem to let go of the fact that everyone knows what happened. I know people are still talking about what Courtney was doing and how we had to send her away. I guess it's partly that I'm embarrassed. But more than anything else, I guess I'm just having to let go of this picture I had of what our family would be like."

As a young parent, you had many pictures. You imagined big events from the first day of school to your daughter's wedding, but you also pictured normal days—sitting around the table, enjoying each other, playing games, trips to the beach, having family devotions.

Some of these pictures may have taken place. Others have not. Your trip to the beach is ruined when one child gets a stomach virus and you have to stay inside the entire week. The first day of school is not what you expected when your child cries all the way to the door of her class. Her wedding is different than what you pictured because of the death of her father last year.

And so it goes. We spend much of our lives letting go of what we picture. Pictures, however, are important. They are a part of the longings we talked about in chapter 6. God uses those pictures to deepen our need for him, but he meets us in the realities. He meets us *even* in the disappointmens of our children not reaching, or even being different from, our expectations. He brings a different picture that is filled with good—even though it is not what we had in our minds.

It is easy to be so disappointed with what's not there that we miss what is. This holds true not only for our lives but also for the girls in them. The mother whose daughter had just come home was so caught up in the past picture that she had trouble rejoicing in her current victories.

Your daughter needs you to dream for her, to picture who she and your family can be. Then she needs you to let go of the picture to see her and love her for who she is.

It is a difficult, courageous job to see your daughter clearly. It takes effort. It takes a willingness to look honestly at your life, to examine your own planks, your expectations, and your needs that wedge their way into your parenting. But as you take this look, the lens starts to clear, and as it does, you are able to see your daughter for who God is uniquely creating *her* to be.

CHAPTER 11

Catching the Vision

All of us need to be in a body that believes we are smarter and better and more gifted than we have ever dared to think we were. For this is one of the ways that each of us will begin to hear the calling voice of God.

Bob Benson, *See You at the House*

When I (Melissa) was a junior in high school, everyone in my class had their hearts set on being in the school play. I was the long shot. My friend Tonda, however, was the actress of our group. She was a shoo-in for the part we were both up for. Tryouts came and Tonda did a fabulous job, while mine was much more mediocre. But when the cast was posted the next morning, I got the part.

Basically, my teacher, Mr. Jeffrey, gave me that part. I knew I didn't deserve it, but for some reason I didn't understand, he saw something more in me. He had a vision, and that spring I worked as hard as I could to be the best actress Murray High had ever seen.

As you think back on your growing up, you may remember a Mr. Jeffrey in your life, someone who believed you were smarter and better and more gifted than you had ever dared to believe. That person had a vision for you. He or she not only saw you as you were but also as you could be.

A vision is a tremendous, impacting gift to give your daughter. It says that you know her. You see who she is with all her strengths and weaknesses. But you also see something more: you see the beginnings of who God is calling her to be.

WHO SHE IS

Who is your daughter? Is she a leader in her class? Is she funny? Is she gifted with animals? Is she weak in math? Does she struggle with friends? Does she feel comfortable with any group she meets? Is she critical of others? Is she tenderhearted? Is she creative? What are her strengths? Her weaknesses?

It is sometimes difficult to see both sides of your daughter. When she has yelled at you or come home after curfew two nights in a row, the weakness side is much more visible. In your exasperation, it is hard to recall her strengths. And when she is doing well—when she is elected the character award at school or scores the winning goal—it is easier to ignore the weaknesses. One looms so large it is difficult to see the other.

We know parents who have a natural propensity toward one side or the other. They naturally focus on their daughter's strengths or her weaknesses—and have a hard time seeing the rest of the girl they love.

The Strength Seer

"My daughter would never do that."

That is the kind of blanket, naive statement that pours forth from the parents who see only strengths. These parents see strengths at the expense of the weaknesses. In essence, they turn a blind eye to the truth about all of who their daughter is, clinging to the parts that give them solace.

These are the parents who see their children as always right and the school or friend or counselor or offending party as always wrong. This parent will assume the best about her daughter without seeing that she is even capable of anything worse.

One of these mothers recently came to us frustrated about her daughter's school. "They have pegged her. They have decided that

Linda is a trouble maker, and so that's all they see. They say she is unkind to other kids and doesn't try in school. But I know she does. For some reason, they're out to get her. It seems as if they're out to get our whole family."

Two things can happen to this child. First, she starts to see herself as the victim. She truly believes she is an innocent recipient of all the harm that other people inflict on her. She doesn't learn to see herself as a responsible, sometimes hurtful party in her own right.

A second thing a girl with this kind of parent can start to believe is that her mother or father doesn't really know her. We hear girls say often, "My mom tells me I'm pretty—but she has to. She's my mom."

Girls are perceptive. They know when we compliment them to make them feel better. As we have talked about before, they know the truth about themselves, and when we skip over that truth, they don't feel that we know them. Our compliments fall on deaf ears.

The Weakness Seer

Daniel only sees his sixteen-year-old daughter's weaknesses. He tells her that she is selfish, that she needs to spend more time with the family, and that she should appreciate all that her parents do for her. After all, her father insists, they are living in a home, not running a hotel.

Daniel's frustrations are shared by many parents of teenagers. It is especially difficult to see your daughter's strengths when she is in her Narcissistic Years (see chapter 4). It feels impossible to point out the good in her when she is selfish or angry or disobedient. Those parts of her are so painful, so disappointing, that they become all many parents see.

This child will often become angry. Because she can't get the positive attention she longs for from her parents, she will take any attention she can. She will act out even more. She will do whatever it takes to get noticed by her mom or dad.

She also may give up. Knowing she can't please her parents, she will stop trying. An adolescent girl recently told us her father called her a prostitute because of the way she dressed. Today, she sneaks out of her room every night to meet a different boy. It's not for money ... yet. But she definitely believes she can gain the approval from a boy that she can't get from her father. She has given up on him.

Seeing the Strengths and the Weaknesses

There is more to your daughter than just her strengths or her weaknesses. She is a mixed-up, overflowing, messy amalgam of both. At times, one will stand out, and at times, the other will be more significant. For her to catch your vision for her, she needs to know that you see *both* her strengths and her weaknesses.

I (Sissy) was a great con artist growing up. I was (and still can be) great at convincing people I was kind, competent, and resourceful—and people believed me. I was elected president of various clubs and chosen "Most Friendly" of my senior class. But I knew the truth. I knew that I was selfish more often than I was kind. I knew I was impatient, critical, and often angry.

As a result, many of the accolades I received fell on deaf ears. I wanted someone to see who I was at my best and at my worst—and still believe in me. I wanted someone to love me in spite of myself, rather than because of the things I accomplished.

When I was growing up, we lived next to the Longs, a family who did just that. They loved me and teased me at the same time. They were unimpressed by offices or awards. To them, I was Sissy. I don't think anyone else in my life lovingly called me a brat during those years except the Longs, and I couldn't be more thankful for that dear family.

Your daughter knows who she is. She knows that she is made

up of both strengths and weaknesses, and she needs you to know these things too. For her to believe in who you say she can be, she needs to know that you see her fully as she is.

WHO SHE CAN BE

> *"You all talk about this whole vision thing all the time. I don't really get what you're saying. My daughter drives me crazy. She's selfish. She yells instead of speaks to me. She has no regard for anyone in our family. How in the world am I supposed to see past all of that? How do you suggest I have a vision for her when she's acting like that?"*

A friend and I (Sissy) actually had this conversation in a grocery store a few years ago. Her daughter was in the middle of her Narcissistic Years, and her mother had lost all sight of how to help her. She knew her daughter felt bad about herself; she knew she was struggling with friends, but because of the way this daughter treated her and her brother, this single mom was at the end of her rope. She couldn't drum up compassion for her daughter—let alone a vision.

She's right. Visions are hard, hard work. They are much easier for counselors, teachers, and coaches who are not living in your home with you. But for parents who are in middle of the messy, chaotic, emotionally turbulent teenage years, they can feel next to impossible.

You may be asking the same questions as this frustrated mom. "What are you saying? What *is* a vision? And how in the world do I have one?"

We would define a *vision* as "a picture of who your daughter can be that God brings about as you attend to him with hope, persistence, and trust." Doesn't sound very easy, does it? That's why the work is God's rather than yours. The vision is caught by you, rather than created. There are four main elements to this work that will help you catch the vision we believe God wants to give you for the girl you love:

- Pray!
- Listen
- Assume the best
- Stay the course

Pray!

Visions are caught, rather than created. Several years ago I (Melissa) taught at camp on this idea of visions. The kids' response was much like Sissy's friend in the grocery store. I talked about it for about an hour that night and explained it pretty thoroughly, and then I told the kids that I wanted them to tell each other their visions for each other.

Pandemonium ensued. Twenty high school voices were nervously and loudly saying things like, "What? I have no idea how to do that. I don't know what to say. You've got to be kidding."

I told them that I wanted them to be quiet and pray. I wanted them to trust that God would give them a vision for their friends, and after several loud sighs and a few minutes, he did.

Celia, who is now known for her ability to have visions for those she loves, got the ball rolling: "John, I have a vision for you. I see you as an adult who people want to be around. They feel comfortable and safe when they're around you, a lot like we do now. So, I see you ..." she closed her eyes and lifted her head, "... I see you grilling barbecue chicken in your backyard. You have two sons and one daughter chasing each other around you. Your wife is making lemonade, and your friends are gathered talking, enjoying being at your house and being around you."

Celia's vision for John was very specific, probably more specific than the vision God wants to give you for your daughter.

Your vision will most likely be more about who God is calling her to be than what she will be doing in her backyard at age thirty. But Celia's vision caught on. She prayed and *God gave her* a picture of who John could be that he brought about as she attended to God with hope, persistence, and trust.

As a parent, you have most likely already caught this vision. You caught it as she twirled in her dress outside as a four-year-old wanting to show God how pretty she was. You caught it as she gave a flower to your elderly neighbor. Your vision for her, as a child, had to do with the tenderness and sensitivity that God had so clearly placed inside her.

But then, she hit adolescence ... and you lost that vision. It's hard to remember the tenderness past the grunts and explosions. It feels much more complicated than simply praying for a vision, but we know that God can help you re-catch that vision for your child.

A frustrated mother came into my (Sissy's) office last fall in tears. "My fifteen-year-old daughter, Skyler, acts like she hates me. All she does is yell at me. It doesn't matter if I'm trying to be kind to her or discipline her. I'm so tired. Part of me just wants to give up.

"But then I pray. Every time I do, I know God is telling me to hang on. This is not who Skyler is—and the funny thing is that I keep having flashes of memories of Skyler as a little girl. It's as if he wants me to know that all of that sweetness is still inside of her, and I know it can come out. As much as I want to at times, I am not going to give up. She may not be willing to change right now, but I can. I want to do whatever it takes to help her become an older version of that little girl I remember."

The best thing this mother did for her daughter was pray. Her prayer helped her re-catch her vision for Skyler, and it helped her have confidence in her parenting. She knew she was right to give Skyler consequences when she was not being the Skyler her mother knew she could be, and the prayer helped her have patience in God's work and his timing.

Skyler came to camp this summer and accepted Christ. When her mother came to pick her up at the end of the week, we told her about Skyler's decision. Her eyes immediately filled with tears. "I haven't been able to get Skyler off my mind this week. I have been praying for her and for all of you constantly."

Skyler's mother re-caught a vision for her, through prayer. God reminded her of who Skyler was and, in that, who he had made her to be. Skyler is still becoming. She is not yet an older version of that little girl, but her mother's prayers are making a huge difference in that direction.

Visions are a mystery. We couldn't conjure one up if we tried. But God wants you to see who he is creating your daughter to be. He wants to show you the good—the unique giftedness he has placed inside her.

Listen

A study called *Experiencing God* took the Christian community by storm in the early 1990s. It talked about seeing what God is doing, and joining him there. At times, *we* want to decide what God is doing. Our wishful thinking almost makes us assume that God wants one thing in our lives and in our parenting when he may actually want something different.

Several years ago I (Sissy) counseled a young woman whose father had told her that God called her to be a Christian singer. She was definitely gifted. She had the talent to pull it off, but in her heart, she wanted to be a veterinarian.

She didn't know what to do with her dad (who, as a side note, was planning on being her manager). She didn't want to disappoint him, but she felt God was calling her somewhere else.

The kind of vision we're talking about in this chapter is not so much about what God has called your daughter to do with her life as it is about who he has called her to be. It is a vision that only comes through prayer—asking God for that vision and listening to receive it.

What do you feel God is doing in the life of your daughter? Where has he uniquely gifted her? How is he using those gifts today? Where can you imagine him using them in the future?

God is doing something in the life of your daughter, whether she is an active participant in a youth group or is saying she doesn't believe in him. He still believes in her and has placed profound gifts in her life.

Watch her as she interacts with her friends. Be a student of how she lives. Notice the subtle ways she responds to hard things ... and hard people. You will see more of who she is as you watch her and as you listen to God.

In the listening, you find sturdier ground. You are not as tossed about with the ups and downs of her adolescent moodiness; you are able to have an abiding trust in God's plan for her, rather than your own; and you are able to hear and see who he is creating her to be.

In the class we offer for parents of girls, we have a group of adolescent girls come to the final session. During this class, the parents and grandparents in the audience are permitted to ask any question they would like of the girls. Recently a young mother asked every girl to name something their mothers had done that they believe had made a difference in their lives.

Five out of five girls talked about their mother's relationship with Christ. (They were asked specifically about what their mothers had done in response to the question.) One girl talked about waking early throughout her life to see her mother in the kitchen with her Bible and a cup of coffee. Another girl talked about knowing that her mother prayed for her daily. Yet another talked about knowing that her mother really sought the Lord's guidance in decisions for their family.

In other words, the mothers of these girls listened. The young mother who asked the question came up to us after class, more than a little overwhelmed, and said, "I know what girls need for a mom—they need a spiritual rock."

To have heard these teenage girls talk, their moms did sound like spiritual rocks, but we know each of these moms well. They are not spiritual rocks. They are moms who deeply and imperfectly love their daughters and who, even more importantly, want to listen so that their parenting can be guided by their own dependence on God.

Assume the Best

After counseling several years, you start to see the same family come in every so often. They are not exactly the same family—they have different names and different combinations of children, but the dynamics are the same.

One such family we see regularly has a daughter we will call Dr. Jekyll/Miss Hyde. This girl is typically a teenager. She is a joy to work with. After a few sessions, it's hard to remember why she is even in counseling. But then we meet with her parents.

"Liz has probably told you everything is fine. She loves school, has great friends, and has a happy family. Well, most of that is true. She does love school and has a lot of friends. She makes good grades and her teachers love her. But she is a monster at home. It's like she stores it all up for us. She comes home and doesn't speak. She goes straight to her room, and if we even make a noise like we want to be with her, she erupts. Everyone in our home walks on tiptoes around Liz."

There are several dynamics going on with girls like Liz. Her parents are right, in many ways. She most likely is storing things up for home. She feels that she has to be friendly and kind at school in order to be liked, but she can only keep up that energy for so long. However she has had her feelings hurt or been disappointed during the day all comes out when she gets home. This is definitely a problem. But the main problem is Liz's perception of what it takes to be liked.

We want Liz to see that she is more than just her friendliness and constant smile. There is much about her that is likable. What is happening, however, is a self-fulfilling prophecy: Liz feels that people will like her only if she is sweet and kind. So Liz is that way at school and then is not that way at home—and what happens at home? Her family doesn't like her. They see her as an angry monster stomping around their home. She knows this. She senses how they see her and starts to see herself that way. Visions, by nature, are catching.

Right now, Liz's family assumes the worst about her. They assume she is angry and purposely saves all that anger for them. This keeps that self-fulfilling ball rolling. Like the mom in the grocery store, Liz's family can't find compassion or a vision to offer her.

But they could start to assume the best. They could start to believe that Liz does not intentionally store up her anger. Maybe Liz is really hurting. Maybe she has felt enough rejection at school that she is panicked to keep up a good face to make others like her. That is a tremendous amount of pressure for a teenage girl. If her parents could start to see this in Liz, they might be able to draw forth some compassion.

The compassion helps her parents see Liz as more of a girl than a monster. They can still help her deal with her hurt at school and her anger at home, but they would assume the best about Liz rather than the worst, and this kind of conversation could follow: "Liz, we know things must be really hard at school. You probably feel as tired of the anger as we do. We want to help. We want to take you to talk to someone who can help you see yourself as we see you—as a lovable, kind, strong mess who doesn't have to be controlled by pleasing people or by your anger, and then we need to deal with things at home. We want to help you with how you feel and we want to help you stop taking it out on us. We know you probably don't even know when you're doing it. So we're going to ground you when it happens, to help you break the cycle. Like you, we really hate to do all this, but we do want to help you feel free."

Liz's parents will still give her consequences, but they will assume the best about her as they give them. They are seeing past who she is to who she can be.

Once again, this idea of assuming the best can sound impossible. You may be facing the death of one of your own parents, coping with the betrayal of a spouse, or even just dealing with the laundry for an entire household. Any of these tasks can make assuming the best feel impossible—and it is. At least, it's impossible without the first two points included in this chapter: prayer and listening.

By nature, we often assume the worst, but as we pray and listen to God, he can quiet our own critical voices. He can help us see past our own issues and insecurities. He can help us see our daughter through his eyes, so that we can re-catch his vision for her.

Stay the Course

Visions are not only hard to attain, they are hard to maintain. You may have prayed, listened, and assumed the best about your daughter, but then you get a call from the police that they have caught her stealing and have taken her to juvenile hall for the night. The vision shatters.

You are finally beginning to hear how God has placed inside her a sensitivity and awareness of others. You can see how he is using her in the lives of other kids in her school who are outsiders. Then, as you are walking by her room, you hear her call one of those kids a "bitch" on the phone. Where is her sensitivity now? How do you believe the best?

You do it by staying the course. Your daughter is becoming who God has created her to be. She is not there yet. The vision will come only as glimpses during these years, and then it will disappear, much like it does in all of us. Don't give up on her, and never give up on what God is doing inside her. He is bringing about his vision for her. He is calling you to catch it. Even when the worst happens that you can imagine, God and the good he has planned for your daughter are not lost. Stay the course.

Visions are a mystery. They are a mystery in that we have nothing to do with their creation. But they are also a mystery in that they are catching. God wants to give you his vision for your daughter, and when the vision becomes fuzzy, he wants to give it to you again.

What happens, over time, is that she starts to catch on. As you see her gifts, she starts to see them too. As you believe she is talented, or kind, or funny, or tenderhearted, she does, too. She catches your vision—God's vision for her.

CHAPTER 12

Enjoying Each Other?

Nobody will listen to you unless they sense that you like them.

DONALD MILLER, *BLUE LIKE JAZZ*

Bras spinning on a ceiling fan are not my (Sissy's) idea of enjoyment, but they were a huge source of fun for several teenage girls last summer. After a particularly long day at camp, I was thrilled to be climbing into my bed at last. As I closed my eyes, I heard whoops of laughter coming from the next room—the room next to mine and also next to the room where eighteen second through fourth graders had just fallen asleep. I was up and through the door quickly.

What I found was five of our leadership girls, who are the kids we believe in and trust to be examples to our younger kids at camp, sitting on the floor laughing hysterically as their bras spun around the ceiling fan.

How do you enjoy your girls when their idea of enjoyment is completely different from yours? Or when they simply feel un-enjoyable? I sure didn't know that night. I think my look communicated all that I didn't say, and I went straight back to bed.

There will be bra-spinning moments for all of us who love girls. There will be times that we simply cannot muster up the energy or don't feel that it would even be helpful for us to enter into their enjoyment.

But there are other times too. There are days when you will see a double rainbow together on a walk, or you will teach her to ride her bike for the first time, or you will simply share a really good laugh. Your daughter needs these times, as author Donald Miller says, to know that you like her, and you need these times—to reinforce what you're wanting to see happen in your relationship and, sometimes, for you to remember that you like her.

THE POWER OF ENJOYMENT

Think back over your teachers from school. Which ones do you remember? Who made the most positive impact on you? We would guess that the ones who made the most difference weren't necessarily the smartest or the strictest or even the ones everyone considered the "coolest," but the ones who seemed to like you.

These teachers made us want to read or write or work harder in class. We wanted to help them with bulletin boards and made sure our moms got them the best Christmas gift. What endeared us to these teachers had more to do with the way they treated us than it had to do with their teaching skills. Even at young ages, we sensed that these teachers enjoyed us, and enjoyment helps all of us feel liked.

We tell interns at Daystar that sometimes the very best thing you can offer a child or teenager is simply to enjoy them. Kids who feel enjoyed are more prone to listen, to respond, and to begin to feel that there could be something enjoyable about themselves.

It's easy for us to say, though. We simply turn our girls back to their parents after an hour of counseling or a week of camp. You are with her through much harder situations than bras and ceiling fans. You are there to hear her shout, "I hate you!" You are there when she slams her door over and over. Especially during adolescence, you are with her during most of the worst and, it feels like, very little of the best.

OBSTACLES TO ENJOYMENT

You finally have some free time in the afternoon to sit down with your six-year-old and play her favorite board game—and the phone rings. It's your mother calling to tell you about her friend who has just been diagnosed with cancer. The game and the enjoyment are put on hold ... again.

It's been way too long since you've done anything where you and your thirteen-year-old actually had fun together. So you tell her that you will take her shopping after school. She seems excited—and then after school comes. You see her scowl before she even reaches the carpool line. She gets in the car and won't speak to you. No explanations, no smiles, and definitely no "I'm so excited to go with you shopping, Moms." How do you enjoy that?

We have found that there are universal obstacles to enjoyment—for you and for her. These obstacles have a knack of knowing just the right time to show up and stop you both from enjoying the gifts God has given you in each other. In the next section, "The Bare Necessities," we'll speak to what you can do about these obstacles, but for now, we want to identify exactly what the obstacles are—for her and for you.

Obstacles for You

"If I don't do it, who will?"

This sentence stops many parents in their tracks.

Your nine-year-old is tugging at your sleeve to get you to play tennis with her. All you see are the mounting dishes in the kitchen and bills on your desk, with no one else who is capable or willing to help.

Your twelve-year-old wants you to go to a movie with her on Sunday afternoon, but you also know that she needs you to help her pack for camp and sew her name in all her clothes. She sure can't do those things. How do you do both?

Children need to feel enjoyed by you, but they also need to be woken up, fed, driven to school, picked up from school, taken to practices, fed again, helped with homework, told good-night, and much more in between. We're telling you to enjoy her, but you also know that she depends on you to provide for her. Often, the two seem mutually exclusive. What do you do?

"I have too much to do to think about fun"

There simply are not enough hours in the day. You would love to enjoy your daughter ... and your son ... and your spouse ... and your friends ... and your terribly neglected dog. No one feels like they are getting enough time with you. And you aren't getting much time to yourself!

You work nine, sometimes ten hours in a day. You leave for work before the kids wake up and often come home just as they are getting into bed. There is barely enough time for a bedtime story. Balancing a career, a marriage, children, a social life, a relationship with God (not necessarily in that order) can make enjoyment feel like an addition to a very long list. You'll get to that next week ... or month.

What do you do? How do you find time to enjoy your child in the midst of all of the chaos of your daily life?

"She doesn't appreciate anything I do anyway"

I (Sissy) remember with remarkable clarity a comment my grandmother made when I was in elementary school. Hedy was a very generous woman, but that generosity had limits. "Sugar Babe," she said, "people like to be thanked. Thank-you notes help them feel like you appreciate what they've done for you. People who are not thanked eventually stop giving gifts."

After we had that conversation, I made sure to write my grandmother a thank-you note for every present I received from her—

big or small—but I sure didn't write them to my parents. They were supposed to give me gifts. They were my parents.

It is a rare thing for a daughter to express gratitude toward her parents. She sees you in much the same way I saw my parents. I knew they loved me and would do anything for me—but that was their job. Why would I thank them? (Mom and Dad, I do appreciate you both immensely.)

Especially in their adolescent years, girls are narcissistic, and today more than ever before, they feel a sense of entitlement. Of course she gets a cell phone and an iPod and a laptop and a car when she turns sixteen. That's just the way things are.

When your daughter lives with this kind of entitlement, it can be difficult to enjoy her. You take her on a trip, and she never says thank you. Not only is she ungrateful, but she barely speaks to you while you're there. You take several of her friends to lunch so that you can enjoy being a part of her world, and she makes fun of you in front of them. How do you enjoy her then?

"I don't know how to enjoy her now that she's a teenager"

It is much easier to enjoy your daughter when she wants to spend time with you. When she's in elementary school, you can bake together or play games or go for walks. She holds your hand and tells you that she loves you.

Then she hits thirteen. She would not be caught dead holding your hand, and she sure doesn't want to spend time with you. She grunts when you suggest that you go somewhere as a family. She laughs when you ask her to play a game.

What do you do? How do you find something she will actually do with you—other than argue—now that she is a teenager?

"I don't enjoy anything she enjoys. How do we enjoy each other?"

Her sense of humor consists of sarcasm and body noises. She laughs when other people fall down or look foolish. None of that is funny to you.

She enjoys loud music. She has fun when she's with her friends—very far away, it seems, from you. She likes to skateboard and draw Japanese animation ... not anything you would necessarily do in your free time.

How do you enjoy your daughter when, on the surface, you have nothing in common other than your last name? How can you find something fun to do together?

Obstacles for Her

"My parents are boring—they don't do anything fun"

It's amazing how many children believe this about their parents, and sadly, there are parents who will admit they stop having time for fun when they have children.

I (Melissa) met with a mom recently who was struggling with her adolescent daughter. I told her that I wanted her to enjoy life outside of parenting, since being a parent currently was not the source of much enjoyment for her. "When was the last time you and your husband went on a trip without the kids?" I asked her.

"I can't remember."

"When was the last time you went out, just the two of you?"

"Well, between soccer games and dance practices, we really have to be home with the kids. There just isn't much time ..." Her next sentence was, "I know—we're so boring."

Even this mother felt that their life had become tedious. She and her husband didn't enjoy themselves, unless it was vicariously through their children.

This happens so often with parents, and understandably so, but it is not as beneficial for your child as you might believe. She needs to see that you have a life outside of her. For her to understand that she can enjoy you, she needs to see that you can enjoy yourself.

"I don't enjoy anything my parents enjoy. How do we enjoy each other?"

This statement is often true, which is why it's the only obstacle included in both sections. You often don't have the same interests. You would not choose the same activities on a free Saturday afternoon.

So what do you do? You compromise. You invite her to enjoy you, which we'll talk about in the next section, and you learn to care about at least a few of the things she does.

If she loves to draw Japanese animation (*anime*, as it is known among its followers), learn to appreciate anime. You don't have to draw it yourself to enjoy her affinity for it. If she plays lacrosse, ask her to show you how to throw the ball with her stick.

Her interests don't have to become yours. You can learn to appreciate her appreciation for them. You can enjoy her determination, her talent. You can help to call out who she is even as she listens to hard-core rock music. She could tell you about her favorite bands—without you ever having to listen to them.

Be a student of what she loves but continue to love your own things too. She needs this as much as you do.

"All my dad does is lecture me; there's nothing to enjoy"

We hear this comment from girls of all ages ... about both parents. They don't feel liked, so they don't listen. But they also are full to the brim of information and instruction.

A father told us, "I only get to be with my daughter every so often. I have to make every minute count. There is too much for her to learn."

It is a gift for you to pass on your wisdom to your daughter, but the lessons need to be shorter rather than longer as she gets older. Her attention span wanes with every year she moves toward teenagedom.

Enjoyment helps her listen and respond to what you have to offer. It also helps her feel that you understand her. Teach your daughter, but enjoy her too. You both need breaks from the intensity of your relationship so you can enjoy it.

THE BARE NECESSITIES OF ENJOYMENT

Before you read any farther, try to remember as many of the lyrics of the song "The Bare Necessities" (from Disney's *Jungle Book*) as you can. Whistle it, hum it, sing it—whatever you have to do to remember what good old Baloo the bear was trying to teach Mowgli.

We sang it together as we tried to remember the words. Not only did our dogs look at us a little strangely, but we ended up laughing and enjoying ourselves. That was Baloo's point.

It's difficult to feel your frustrations with your daughter and enjoy her at the same time. Your frustration may still be there, but the enjoyment usurps it. The wise, old bear tells Mowgli to "forget about your worries and your strife."

That is hard to do at times, as a parent—especially if you are concerned about or frustrated with your daughter. But she still needs you to enjoy her, and we have a few bare necessities of our own to make the enjoyment a little easier.

Take a Step Back—Rest

Sometimes our worst enemy is not a person but our own imaginings. Your daughter goes straight to her room after school—she doesn't like you anymore. She chooses to go on vacation with a friend's family rather than yours—she thinks they're more fun. She yells at you for asking her a question—she hates you and wants to trade you in for a different mother.

These imagined messages you think your daughter is sending you can start to control your thoughts and eventually your behavior toward your daughter. You feel hurt or rejected. Rather than seeing her behavior as a normal part of development, you believe that it has to do with your relationship.

Rest. Most of what your daughter feels has nothing to do with you—even if she tells you it does. Hiccups in self-esteem, problems with friends and boys, longings, hormones—all these contribute to her moodiness. She will, at times, genuinely be angry with you, and then she'll quickly move on to the next thing.

We see parents who feel so hurt by their daughters that the idea of enjoyment sounds impossible. They feel unappreciated, taken for granted, and rejected. Again, we say *rest*. Don't let your imaginings or your hurt control you.

She needs you to enjoy her in the midst of her moodiness. She needs to believe that you can still enjoy yourself when she has hurt you. She wants you to be stronger and bigger than she is. For you to withdraw in pain every time she makes a cutting comment leads her to believe she has too much power.

Jenny's parents are different from some parents. Her mom is sensitive and feels hurt at the tiniest rebuff. Because Jenny is fourteen, these rebuffs come regularly. When they do, her mom withdraws to her bedroom. She ignores Jenny for several hours, wanting her to see how much she has been hurt.

The first time her mom responded in this way, Jenny felt badly. After several rounds of this kind of interaction, however, Jenny stopped caring. Rather than seeing her own behavior as hurtful, she saw her mom as weak.

Jenny's dad, on the other hand, is able to handle things more objectively. Jenny is hurtful to him too, but rather than withdrawing from her, he laughs. When Jenny tells him he is the meanest father in the world, he responds, "Well, Jenny [with a chuckle], it must be awful to have the meanest father in the world for a dad. How do you ever survive?"

And then he walks away. In essence, he's being playful with her. He's pointing out that what she is saying is ridiculous, but he's doing it in a lighthearted and non-accusing way. He does not let her response affect his imaginings.

This kind of rest is hard to come by. It takes a great deal of patience, objectivity, and mostly prayer. But it is possible. Your daughter's moods will come and go, but who she is remains the same. In resting, you are enjoying who you know she is more than what she is acting like right now.

Relax

As you read this paragraph, God is working in your daughter. She might be at the pool with friends or on a date or snuggled safely in bed—but he is working. He's bringing about the woman he has created her to be.

You, obviously, are an important part of this process, but you are not the process. It is not up to you to teach her every learnable lesson before she becomes an adult. She doesn't need you to. What she needs is you to teach and then relax, to believe in her and then to enjoy her.

To enjoy her does not mean your teaching stops. It simply means you are teaching her something different. As you relax and leave the work to God, you are teaching her that he can be trusted, that God has given her many things to be enjoyed. As you find playful outlets together, you are teaching her how to relieve stress, and you are teaching her that relationships involve work *and* play.

Your daughter needs—actually she longs for—you to enjoy her. But to do so means that you must relax. This relaxation comes as you put away many of the obstacles that hinder you. It means you leave the task of organizing the garage to someone else—or for another day. It means that you trust that God is continuing to teach her lessons, even when you aren't the one instructing.

What happens is that she will be more willing to hear your instruction after a little time of enjoyment. Who she is blossoms just as much under your enjoyment as it does under your instruction, and to top it off, she feels liked, understood, and more enjoyable herself.

Play

Briana and Deb came on a mother-daughter retreat with us several years ago. On Saturday afternoon, we had free time to go for a walk, sit on the dock, or play in the yard. Briana and Deb headed straight for the tetherball pole.

Briana was fourteen at the time—energetic, vivacious, and fiercely competitive. Her mom, Deb, was a behind-the-scenes kind of mom. She was a steady source of support and encouragement for all of Briana's endeavors—but things changed with tetherball.

Deb and Briana started whopping that ball back and forth, back and forth, till both of them were breathing hard. We're actually not sure if they were breathing hard from exertion or from laughter. We all saw a side of Deb that day we had never seen before—including Briana.

This is not the norm for many parents. I (Sissy) remember having a friend over to play in grade school. We sat down on the floor to play Candy Land, and my mom sat down with us. My friend whispered, "Why is your mom on the floor?" When I told her she was going to play with us, my friend was shocked. She said her mom never played games with her and would certainly not sit on the floor.

My friend's mom lived as many parents do. You swim with your daughter while you're teaching her, but then you stop getting in the pool. You snow ski with her to show her how, and then you're ready to call it a day. You play tennis with her but concentrate more on her swing than on your enjoyment of the game.

In teaching girls to have fun, you forget to have fun yourself. You lose your own sense of play in creating playful opportunities for them. It is part of your job to create and to teach, but it is also your job to rest, relax, and play.

When Deb sent that tetherball right back to Briana as hard as Briana had hit it, Briana was surprised. She was used to her mom enjoying her. But as Deb's own playful spirit came to life, she invited Briana to enjoy her back. In those moments, Briana's mom became more than just her steady, supportive mom. She became her own person.

You don't have to invite her to enjoy you in ways that don't fit who you are. Part of the reason for the invitation is for her to see your personality. Remember what you loved, maybe even before you had children. Drive her to the park you used to play in as a girl and swing with her. If you are snow skiing together, be the one to create a path through the trees. Race her to the car when you're leaving the mall.

Enjoy your daughter, but let her enjoy you, as well. My (Melissa's) mom has this kind of enjoyment down to an art. On birthdays and holidays she always invites us to enjoy her in ways that are creative and spontaneous. One Christmas we played Christmas carols on glasses filled with different levels of water. On birthdays we had treasure hunts to search for our gifts. Every year, every holiday, we would roll our eyes and say, "Oh, Mom." But secretly we loved it.

We loved the fact that our mom created something fun for us, for all of us to enjoy together. She didn't just watch from the sidelines. She played those glasses right along with us. We enjoyed the adventures. We enjoyed each other in the process. But mostly we enjoyed the creativity and playfulness that she invited us to be a part of.

As you invite them to enjoy, your children will often have the same "Oh, Mom" or "Oh, Dad" kind of responses, but secretly they will love it too. Our message in this chapter is simple: Don't take your daughter *or yourself* too seriously. Rest. Relax. And play. Look for those bare necessities. You all will listen, laugh, and enjoy each other more as a result.

ENJOYMENT AT EVERY STAGE

"Okay," you may be saying, "I get it. I need to let go, enjoy, and invite my daughter to enjoy me. That was easier to do at six than it is at sixteen. What can I do with her now that is enjoyable?"

Development does affect the enjoyment you and your daughter share. It changes as she does. In this section, we'd like to give you a few practical ideas of how to enjoy your daughter at every stage. Some of these ideas are ours, and some come directly from the girls you are hoping to enjoy.

The Discovery Years—Birth to Five

- In her first year, smile at her—make faces and sounds that make her laugh
- Get on the floor and play games with her
- Join her in role-playing types of games where you are the child and she is the mommy or the daddy or the teacher
- Play outside with her—swing, do forward rolls in the yard, go for walks
- Take her to the pool or to a playground
- Read picture books to her
- Wrestle and tickle her
- Play in the sprinkler with her
- Sing and dance with her
- Laugh and laugh and laugh

The Adventurous Years—Six to Eleven

- Take her to do some type of physical activity like horseback riding, water- or snow-skiing
- Help her learn to paint or to draw. If you're not artistic, take an art class with her
- Have her teach you the gymnastics she is learning in class
- Bake cookies or brownies together for a sick neighbor

- Read books out loud with her—taking turns reading
- Make an adventure out of a family vacation—do something unusual and surprise her
- Make decorations for the Christmas tree together
- Have pillow fights with her
- Go to the humane society and choose a family pet together
- Camp out in the back yard
- Take her fishing or hiking

The Narcissistic Years—Twelve to Fifteen

- Go for walks around the neighborhood
- Show her some of your favorite movies from when you were younger and have her show you hers
- Fix a family meal together
- Take her on a mother-daughter or father-daughter trip to shop, see a play, or go canoeing
- Go on a surprise run to Starbucks or Dairy Queen
- Tell her your favorite stories from when she was little
- Look at old family movies together
- Ride bikes together
- Teach her to drive a car
- Take her to the local flea market and bargain hunt for treasures

The Autonomous Years—Sixteen to Nineteen

In these years, she'll enjoy many of the activities she did in the Narcissistic Years, but you can also:

- Take a trip with her where she picks the location (within reason)
- Make a special event out of college visits where you add on a little sightseeing she chooses
- Have her take you shopping

- ☆ Stay up late with her to talk on the porch swing
- ☆ Pick a weekly television show you can enjoy together
- ☆ Take her to a college football or basketball game
- ☆ Volunteer together for a charity you both love
- ☆ Train together for a running, walking, or biking event
- ☆ Redecorate her room together (painting could add to the fun)
- ☆ Play a favorite family game

Whatever her age, there are activities you can choose to enjoy together. But we will add this: don't let her response determine how successful you believe the activity is. Most of the things kids tell us they love to do with their parents are never appreciated in front of the parents themselves. But when she visits her grandparents, then she may tell them how much she enjoyed something she did with her parents. Odds are, she enjoys your activities together more than you know.

CHAPTER 13

Naming Girls

When I was memorizing the names of the stars, part of the purpose was to help them each to be more particularly the particular star each one was supposed to be. That's basically a Namer's job.

MADELEINE L'ENGLE, *A WIND IN THE DOOR*

When your daughter was born, you gave her a name. She may have been named after a family member, a close friend, a Bible verse, or even one of your favorite characters from a book. Regardless of how you chose your daughter's name, you named her. In essence, you said, "This is who you will be to the world," and with that name came all the hopes, expectations, and dreams you had for her.

Before your daughter was born, God gave her a name. His name for her is a secret that will finally be revealed to her in heaven, and his name captures the essence of who he has called her to be. His name says to her, "This is who you are." Before she even knows what that name is, she is growing into it, and that name is calling out in her everything God has uniquely created her to be.

A NAME THAT IS UNIQUE

Our dear friends Pace and Brandon are expecting a baby in September. If the baby is a girl, we have jokingly said she should be named Silissa—the *Si* for Sissy and the *lissa* for Melissa. If nothing else, her name would be unique.

Your daughter's name—her true name—is unique. In this life she may have one of those common names and know five other people in her class who share it, but she is entirely different from all who have come before her or will come after. The name God is calling out in her is hers and hers alone.

You may have hopes for what your daughter's name is. You would like a daughter whose name is "Delightful" or "Woman Beloved by Everyone She Meets," but you may have a daughter named "Creative in Her Solitude" or "Quiet Strength."

As a parent, you do not get to choose the identity of your daughter. She is not a garden in which you can plant zinnia or clematis seeds and watch those particular seeds grow. You will expect poppies and end up with petunias. Why? Because God has already planted the seeds. He chose her name before you even knew of her existence. He has placed an identity inside her that is distinctly hers.

So what is your role? How do you help draw out who God has created your daughter to be? The answer, we believe, lies in author Madeleine L'Engle's quote from *A Wind in the Door*.

A NAMER'S JOB

L'Engle says a namer's job is to "help them each to be more particularly the particular star each one was supposed to be." As a father or mother or grandparent or friend, your job is to help each girl to be more particularly the particular girl she is supposed to be.

God gives her the name, but you help call it out. As Romans 8:17 says we are "co-heirs with Christ," and you are also co-namers of the girl you love. He graciously gives us that place.

We have the mysterious, joyful, precarious honor of discovering who God has called our girls to be. First, we discover this identity God has uniquely sown inside her, and then we help him call it out.

Think about your daughter or granddaughter or student. What characteristics do you see God growing in her? When does she seem most peaceful? When have you seen her have a really good, hard laugh? What brings out her compassion? What draws out her strength? What does she do when she's alone? Where do you see her confidence?

You will spend a lifetime discovering the unique identity God has placed inside of your daughter. You discover her as you lean into him, and her identity will unfold as you listen and watch.

Listen

Your daughter receives a new name every day, and not necessarily a name you would choose to be her identity. You take your daughter to visit your mother-in-law who is recovering from surgery. Rather than telling your daughter how glad she is to see her, she turns to you and says, "Susan sure is quiet these days. She doesn't have as much personality as her sister, does she?" Susan is named in that moment.

You finally persuade your daughter to go with you to look for her prom dress. Browsing through the racks, another mother turns to you both and says, "I am having the same problem you are. They just don't make pretty dresses for big girls." Tragically, your daughter is named.

There are people speaking into your daughter's life every day. Family members, teachers, neighbors, and strangers all speak to the identity they see in your daughter. Some of these individuals will be kind and gracious, and some will be terribly misguided.

And on some days, you will be too. You come home from a long day at work to be greeted by your daughter's adolescent sullenness. The only name you can think to give her is "grump." Your mother has just died, and all your daughter can talk about is what shoes she will wear to the funeral. "Selfish" might seem a little more fitting in this situation.

The names your daughter will hear and the names you will give her will change on a daily basis. Regardless of how or by whom they are spoken, you will hear a bevy of names thrown at your daughter—and you will do some of the throwing yourself.

Listen. It is in the stillness that you will begin to hear God's voice above all the others. His name cuts through the frustrations and the hurtful remarks to remind you of who he is calling her to be.

How do you hear him over the din of other voices? It is in moving out of one world and into another. It is leaving behind the chaos of voices and entering a place of quiet where you can hear. That place is one of prayer.

At times it will be hard to leave the world in which you live. There will always be distractions. And once you start to pray, you may feel that you hear nothing. In those long, discouraging moments, keep praying that God will reveal his heart for your daughter. Pray even when the revealing seems slow. God will answer you in surprising ways.

Watch

It would be helpful if God would walk into your living room and tell you specifically who he has created your daughter to be. Things would make a whole lot more sense. He could explain why she is going through this or that stage, and you would be able to finally say with a sigh of relief, "Oh, now I understand what's happening."

But most likely he won't speak to you in quite this way. He will reveal to you who he has created her to be in the subtleties of who she is rather than in his obvious, direct voice. He will speak it to you in the way she loves a friend who is hurting. He will show you in how she handles herself after a major loss in basketball ... or a victory. He will reveal who she is as she listens to her grandmother's stories and in the way she treats a forgetful waitress.

As you watch your daughter through the years, you will continue to discover who God has named her, and as often happens, when you are looking for a little good, you will likely discover a lot. You will see more and more of the unique characteristics God has placed inside her—and those characteristics all combine to make up her name.

Since you will not know her singular, God-given name, you can name her often from the vastness of all that is welling up inside her.

NAMING THE GIRL YOU LOVE

This book was birthed approximately ten summers ago at a camp where we talked about Revelation 2:17.

> He who has an ear, let him hear what the Spirit says to the churches. To him who overcomes, I will give some of the hidden manna. I will also give him a white stone with a new name written on it, known only to him [or her] who receives it.

This past summer, we revisited this verse with a group of high school juniors and seniors. At the end of camp we gave them new names ... names that were reflective of who we believed God was calling each of them to be.

One of these girls is named Maggie. She has valiantly fought depression and anxiety for the past several years. She's a young woman of tenacious faith, unbridled enthusiasm, and a contagious spirit. To meet Maggie is to enjoy her. The problem was that Maggie no longer enjoyed her own life, and as a result of her depression and anxiety, her light had dimmed.

On the last day of camp, Maggie was given a new name. Her name was Sunrise. The counselor who named her spoke of a light that dispels the darkness. That light is God's spirit that shines so brightly through Maggie ... even in the midst of her depression.

When this counselor named Maggie, she spoke to who she knew Maggie was. Maggie wasn't fully experiencing the sunrise in that moment, but we knew it was there. Maggie was still becoming.

Several months ago, I (Sissy) met with Maggie. We talked about camp. She said that her very favorite part of her week was her new name. When I asked her why, this was her response: "Because it was me. And it was something I'll never forget. I know that God has given me a light to share with others. At times, I don't feel like it. It seems like there is nothing good inside me at all. But that name is always a reminder. I do have a light. I have the light of Christ living inside me, and he put that light there to share with others and to give me hope when things feel dark. I get to shine my light so that other people can experience him. I am a sunrise," Maggie said with a giggle.

In raising girls, we are given a chance to co-name them. Camp and home, however, are obviously different. As a parent, your naming is not a one-time thing. It is something that happens through the raising—and after. You will forever be naming the girl you love.

In these first nineteen years, however, your job as a namer is brought into focus. You name your daughter as you traverse the journey we have outlined in this book. To name her is to see what's normal and what's not in terms of her development, to understand what is going on internally and externally in her world, to look past your own issues to see her clearly, and finally to believe in her and enjoy her. All these things come together to give you more clarity, more depth, and more hope in the naming of the girl you love.

"So how do I do that," you may be asking. "What does it look like for me to name my daughter?" We would say it looks different for every parent, teacher, coach, or adult in the life of a girl, but, here are a few examples of adults who have taken up their jobs as namers.

A father we know takes his daughter for doughnuts for breakfast every Saturday morning—no mommies allowed. In investing this time, he is saying to his daughter, "I notice and value you. I believe you are enjoyable and worthy of my time and undivided attention." He is naming her—helping her become more of the Anna Grace that Anna Grace was specifically made to be—simply by spending time with her and enjoying her.

A mother chose to send her sixteen-year-old-daughter to a therapeutic wilderness program. This young girl was involved in a very destructive relationship with a boy that the mother suspected was becoming abusive, but the daughter didn't have the strength to walk away. Instead, she told more and more lies just to spend time with him. Sending her away was one of the most difficult decisions this mother has ever had to make. But in it, she was naming her daughter. She was saying to her, "You have more strength than you know. I know there is a young woman of honesty and courage inside you, and I am going to do whatever it takes to draw that woman out."

A youth director attends the high school graduation of every child in his youth group, and in all the audience, he is the one who whoops and hollers the loudest. In this small act, he is naming the kids he is there to represent. He is saying, "You are worthy of my time and my admiration. I am proud of who you are becoming."

A grandmother had a surprising response to her granddaughter's sadness over a breakup. She listened late one night as her granddaughter recounted her sad tale, and then she quietly stood up, walked over to the shelf, and pulled out her granddaughter's yearbook. She sat down and started flipping through the pages. "Hmmm. Well, look here." Her granddaughter promptly pulled her chair over to see what her grandmother was commenting on.

What she was doing was naming her granddaughter. She was pointing out all of the other possible "beaus" in her granddaughter's class, and what she was saying was, "You have so much to offer. I think anyone would be lucky to have a date with you."

Naming in real life looks very different than it does at camp. You will probably not speak one word over your daughter's life that changes the course of who she is, but you will have countless opportunities, in little ways, as you walk through these nineteen years with her.

In *A Wind in the Door*, Madeleine L'Engle goes on to describe, from her main character's perspective, what it feels like to be named.

> "Who makes you least confused?"
>
> "Calvin." There was no hesitation there. "When I'm with Calvin, I don't mind being me."
>
> "You mean he makes you more you, don't you?"

God has specifically chosen you for this job of namer. In spite of the fact that you will fail her over and over, he has entrusted you with the life of this girl you love.

As you name your daughter, you help to call out the unique identity God has placed inside her. In doing so, you make her more her. In other words, you help loosen the entanglements of all that holds her back—the insecurities, the rejection from other girls, the confusion with boys—all the turmoil going on inside her and around her.

Your daughter deeply longs for and is created to be in relationship, and your relationship is one that God can use greatly in these nineteen years to impact her for the rest of her life. In the midst of a turbulent, sometimes hurtful world, you can help free her to be more particularly the particular girl she was meant to be.

And that is a pretty terrific job to have.

Afterword by Amy Grant

"It's a girl," the ultrasound nurse declared as she guided the gel-coated device across my belly. My heart skipped a beat. My first-born had been a son, nearly two years before. So far, my only perception of my parenting self was as a boy-mom. I made boys. That's what I did.

This news of a daughter filled me with so much emotion that I couldn't let myself open up to it until I was outside the clinic, standing alone in the parking lot. Then my mind and my heart started to expand, and an unfamiliar and unexpected wave of wonder and relief and gratitude came rushing up from deep inside. I was carrying a baby girl who would one day become a woman. And that woman, if loved and respected, might someday become a friend with whom I could share the rest of my days. A loved woman is an amazing creation, and each has her own "inner mystery," as Maya Angelou describes so well in her poem "Phenomenal Woman."

I wish I had been able to read *Raising Girls* that hot summer day back in 1989 in the wake of my parking lot epiphany. Now, nineteen years later, I am parenting three daughters, and, just as Sissy and Melissa have outlined in their book, the youngest is entering the "Adventurous Stage." The next oldest is fully immersed in the "Narcissistic Years." And my first daughter, the one through whom I have learned so much, is deliberately navigating her way through the "Autonomous Years."

Every chapter of *Raising Girls* brought heartfelt cheers of yes, yes, yes as I read, sometimes laughing out loud, sometimes getting choked up. Parenting is an all-terrain expedition filled with glorious summits and deep dark valleys. As I compared my experiences with the findings of Sissy and Melissa, I marveled at the areas of growth and development that my girls came through with flying colors. How many times had I felt I was flying blind—truly surviving on a wing and a prayer? In other chapters, I winced at the memories of mistakes I'd made in directing my children's lives—faulty thinking on my part ... immaturity.

Life is a steady teacher if we allow it to be. And all of us, through God's mercy and redemption, learn as we go. It's never too late to love our children well. *Raising Girls* has re-inspired me to dream for my daughters, to see their distinctiveness and their potential. I named each of them at birth, and I intend to continue "naming them" with strength and beauty in the way that I love them: through prayer, direction, enjoyment, and respect.

Recommended Reading

Here are just a few of the many terrific books out there that we think you might find helpful.

On Girls

John and Stasi Eldredge, *Captivating*, Nelson, 2005. An insightful book written about women, but it also speaks to the heart and needs of girls.

Michael Gurian, *The Wonder of Girls*, Pocket Books, 2002. A must-read guide to the world of girls.

Sharon Hersh, *Bravehearts*, WaterBrook, 2000. Another helpful book about women that also applies to girls.

———, *Mom, Everyone Else Does!* Shaw, 2005.

———, *Mom, I Feel Fat!* Shaw, 2001.

———, *Mom, I Hate My Life!* Shaw, 2004.

———, *Mom, Sex Is No Big Deal!* Shaw, 2006. All these are part of a practical series dealing with difficult issues girls face.

Amy Lynch and Dr. Linda Ashford, *How Can You* Say *That?* American Girl, 2003. A terrific book that is published by the same company that makes American Girl dolls.

Mary Pipher, *Reviving Ophelia*, Balantine, 1994. A revealing look at girls in our culture from a psychological perspective, taken from her own case studies.

Rachel Simmons, *Odd Girl Out*, Harvest, 2003. A book that gives perspective on the aggressive social world of girls today.

Rosalind Wiseman, *Queen Bees and Wannabees*, Three Rivers Press, 2003. A book that will take you inside the school bathrooms and lunchrooms to what is really going on with girls and between girls.

Notes

Though not specifically footnoted, the following books are referenced in the chapters cited.

Introduction

Barbara Cawthorne Crafton, *The Sewing Room* (Harrisburg, Pa.: Morehouse, 1997), 103.

Michael Gurian, *The Wonder of Girls* (New York: Pocket Books, 2002), 23.

Chapter 1

L. Frank Baum, *The Wizard of Oz* (New York: North-South Books, 1996), 101.

Chapter 2

Mike Mason, *The Mystery of Children* (Colorado Springs: Waterbrook, 2001), 28.

Betty Smith, *A Tree Grows in Brooklyn* (New York: Perennial Classics, 2005), 84.

Anne Lamott, *Operating Instructions* (New York: Fawcett Columbine, 1993), 22.

Chapter 3

Harper Lee, *To Kill A Mockingbird* (New York: HarperCollins, 1960, 1993), 17.

Mary Pipher, *Reviving Ophelia* (New York: Ballantine, 1994), 254.

Chapter 4

Elizabeth Berg, *Durable Goods* (New York: Avon, 1993), 4.

Michael Gurian, *The Wonder of Girls* (New York: Pocket Books, 2002), 38, 78–79.

Chapter 5

Carol Gilligan, *In a Different Voice* (Cambridge, Mass.: Harvard University Press, 1993), 160.

Michael Gurian, *The Wonder of Girls* (New York: Pocket Books, 2002), 89.

Elizabeth Von Arnim, *The Enchanted April*, (London: Virago, 2003), 323–24.

George MacDonald, *The Curate's Awakening* (Minneapolis, Minn.: Bethany House, 1985), 80.

Chapter 6

Sharon Hersh, *Bravehearts* (Colorado Springs: Waterbrook, 2000), 17.

Chapter 7

K. Douglas Wiggins, *Mother Carey's Chickens* (Charleston: BookSurge Classics, LLC, 2004), 25.

Chapter 8

Lucy Maud Montgomery, *Anne of Green Gables* (Philadelphia: Courage Books, 1993), 57.

Chapter 9

Mary Pipher, *Reviving Ophelia* (New York: Ballantine, 1994), 22.

Chapter 10

Richard Rohr, *Everything Belongs* (New York: Crossroad, 2003), 98.

Chapter 11

Bob Benson, *See You at the House* (Nashville: Generoux, 1986), 189.

Chapter 12

Donald Miller, *Blue Like Jazz* (Nashville: Thomas Nelson, 2003), 220.

Chapter 13

Madeleine L'Engle, *A Wind in the Door* (New York: Bantam Doubleday Dell, 1973), 78, 79.

Index

Acknowledgments

At Daystar we talk a lot about gratitude. As we finish this book, our gratitude is overflowing for a group of folks who have been a part of this process with us. Don Pape has been our agent and literary superhero. Sandy VanderZicht is an editor who has challenged us with her kindness and encouraged us with her wisdom. Mimi Heldman has heard our stories, read our drafts, and reminded us of the depth and playfulness bound up in the heart of a girl. Pace Verner has lightened our load with her laughter and been a kind companion along the way. David Thomas, Betsy Cashman, Jeremy Shapiro, Pat McCurdy, Julia Groos, and the Daystar Board have been a steady source of compassionate support throughout this writing process. We have shared meals and girlhood tales with Belle Johnson, Pepper Magargee, and Mary Katharine Hunt, who have continually pointed us toward Christ. Margaret Trevathan (Melissa's mom) has offered her love of life, her love of people, and her humor to us both. Aunt Robbie Stamps has kept us loved and fed. Helen Goff (Sissy's mom) has caught us up on the news and technology and has taught us a great deal about delighting in girls. Bob Goff (Sissy's dad) has taught us the importance of dancing with daughters and an adventure-filled life. Finally, we are grateful for the constant prayers of St. Bartholomew's Church and the family of folks at Daystar Counseling Ministries.

Share Your Thoughts

With the Author: Your comments will be forwarded to the author when you send them to *zauthor@zondervan.com*.

With Zondervan: Submit your review of this book by writing to *zreview@zondervan.com*.

Free Online Resources at www.zondervan.com

Zondervan AuthorTracker: Be notified whenever your favorite authors publish new books, go on tour, or post an update about what's happening in their lives.

Daily Bible Verses and Devotions: Enrich your life with daily Bible verses or devotions that help you start every morning focused on God.

Free Email Publications: Sign up for newsletters on fiction, Christian living, church ministry, parenting, and more.

Zondervan Bible Search: Find and compare Bible passages in a variety of translations at www.zondervanbiblesearch.com.

Other Benefits: Register yourself to receive online benefits like coupons and special offers, or to participate in research.